PYTHON FOR

BEGINNERS:

Table of Contents

Introduction

Basics of Programming

Before we take a plunge into the world of computer programming, let us take a closer look at what computer programs are and what they are supposed to be. The standard defining of a computer program is as follows:

> A sequence of instructions for performing a particular task that has been written in a specific programming language is commonly referred to as a computer program.

As you can see in the given definition, two phrases have been written in bold namely, 'sequence of instructions' and 'programming language'. To understand the meaning and significance of these two terms, let us take an example. For instance, you have a household help and you have to tell her the procedure to prepare 2 cups of coffee. What will be the set of instructions that you will give to her? In all probability, you will tell her something like this –

1. Firstly, take two cups and keep them on the kitchen slab.

2. Take a boiling pan and using one of these cups for measurement, add two cups of water to it.

3. Switch on the stove.

4. Put the boiling pan on medium heat and wait until the water starts boiling.

5. In the two cups, add 1 teaspoon of coffee, 1 teaspoon of sugar and 1 teaspoon of milk powder.

6. Add boiling water to the cups.

7. Lastly, serve.

The seven steps mentioned above form what can be called 'human program'. It is a set of instructions that you have given to a human to perform a specific task. Since the language used for this human program is English, the programming language used for writing this human program is English. If your household help doesn't understand English, this human program will fail. Therefore, you will have to translate this program to the language she understands, which can be French, Arabic, Hindi, Spanish or any other language for that matter.

Analogously, when you have to tell the computer to do something for you, you have to give it a set of instructions in the language that it can understand. The language that it understands is the computer programming language and the set of instructions written in that language and given to the computer to perform a specific task is simply a computer program.

There are some other terms that you may also encounter in the world of computer programming. One such term is software. A computer program is usually also referred to as software. Besides this, you may also see phrases like source code and program coding. These are terms usually used for referring to the set of instructions written in a computer program.

Computer Programs

Computer programs are the heart and soul of a computer. The hardware is just a dead body unless you have active computer programs running on the system. All the capabilities of the computer can be used only after you tell the computer what it should do for you in the form of computer programs.

We unconsciously use many computer programs everyday. For instance, Google Chrome or Internet

Explorer that you use to browse Internet is a computer program. The chat programs you use on your computer or mobile phone is a computer program. Moreover, the voice calls and SMS capabilities of mobile phones are also computer programs. You name it and there is a computer program associated with it. Whenever and whenever you use a computer to do a task, you are using a computer program.

Since computer programming is a skilled job, the individual who has an expertise in computer programming is referred to as a computer programmer. Depending on the programming language in which the computer programmer has expertise, he or she is called Python/C/HTML/Java/CSS/SQL/JavaScript programmer.

Algorithm

Now that you are thorough with the concept of computer program, you can simply relate computer programming to the process and art of writing computer programs. These programs should not only perform the specified task, but they should also do them well. This is where the concept of effective and efficient programming came into existence.

In order to make the process of program designing simpler, several approaches have been designed. The systematic procedure developed to solve a problem is called an algorithm. It is one of the most effective approaches for creation of a sequence of well-defined instructions aimed towards performing a task. You will hear this term just as much as you shall counter computer programs as they essentially go hand in hand.

In simple words, an algorithm is an English language equivalent of the computer program, written in the form of a list, by the programmer, before transforming it into a programming language – specific code. A sample algorithm has been given below to help you understand how an algorithm typically looks like. This algorithm given below computes the largest number from a list of numbers.

Algorithm for Computing Largest Number From Given List of Numbers

1. Get the given list of numbers.

2. **Assume a variable L, which will hold the largest number.**

3. Initialize L with the first number of the list.

4. Go to the next number of the list.

5. If L is less than this number, put this new number in L

6. Repeat step 4 and step 5 till the list is completely scanned.

7. Print L on the screen

This is a raw algorithm written in simple language to make it easy to understand for beginners. There is a standard procedure that needs to be followed for writing algorithms. However, this is part of advanced programming fundamentals and is beyond the scope of this book.

Programming Languages

Just like we have innumerable languages that are used for communication between humans, scientists have developed a plethora of computer programming languages to serve and meet the varied requirements of developers and applications. We will introduce some of the key languages to you in the chapters to come. A list of the programming languages that we shall cover is as follows –

1. Java

2. **SQL**

3. C

4. C++

5. C#

6. Python

7. HTML

8. **<u>CSS</u>**

9. **JavaScript**

In order to understand the concept of programming languages, their structure and how they work, let us look at English, which is a standard human interface language. It is used by billions of people around the world to communicate with each other. As we know, English language makes words from a set of alphabets and these words are used to make sentences.

In order to make sure that the sentences are understandable to one and all, several grammar rules have to be applied. Besides this, language elements like conjunctions, verbs, nouns and adverbs, in addition to several others, have to be kept in mind while forming sentences. Likewise, other languages like French, Spanish, Russian, Arabic or Hindi also have their own set of rules that need to be followed for effective communication between two humans.

In the same manner, computer languages also have rules and elements that need to be understood before you can write programs to communicate with the computer. Some of these basic elements are as follows –

- Syntax
- Data types
- Keywords
- Variables
- Operators
- Loops
- Decision Making
- Program organization elements like Functions
- File I/O
- Programming environment

Most of the languages that we shall deal with in this book will have most of these elements. However, how they are included in the programming language varies. In this book, we shall introduce you to the different programming languages listed above and deal with the different elements and advanced programming concepts specific to the programming language in books specifically written for the language.

Chapter 1: Programming Environment

Although, programming environment does not form one of the core elements of a programming language, it would not be wrong to state that it is one of the prerequisites that you need to learn and get acquainted with even before you have written your first program. You will never know if your program is right or wrong unless you have a programming environment that can test the same for you. This is the reason why we are going to introduce you to programming environment before we jump to languages.

Simply, programming environment is software that will allow you to create, compile and execute computer programs on the system. It is an interface between the programmer and the computer, which will convert the programs that you will write into the computer's language and ask it to execute the same for you. Therefore, before you pick up any programming language, be sure to enquire about the required programming environment and how the same can be set up on the computer that you intend to use for your programming course.

Digging deeper into the programming environment and its setup, it is made up of three basic elements namely text editor, compiler and interpreter. In all probability, you will need all these three components for your course. So, before you go searching for them, let us help you understand what they exactly are and why you will need them.

Text Editor

A text editor is a simple text program that will allow you to create text files in which you will write you code. Depending on the programming language you are working on, the extension of the text file will change. For instance, if you programming in C language, your text files will have the extension .c.

If you are working on a Windows machine, you can simply search for Notepad in the search bar and use it as a text editor for your programs. You can also explore Notepad++ for some advanced options. It is freely available and you will just need to download and install it on your machine. On the other hand, if you are a Mac user, you can explore text editor options like BBEdit and TextEdit.

Compiler

Now that you have written the program and you are all ready to test if you have written it correctly or not, you have to give it to the computer and see if it understands what you are trying to communicate. However, the computer only understands binary language and what you have written is far from what it can directly digest. Therefore, this file needs to be converted into binary format.

If you have made syntactical errors and not followed the rules of the programming language, the compiler will not be able to make this conversion smoothly and will raise an error message for you. Therefore, the compiler is a program that checks if you have followed the syntactical rules of the chosen programming language and converts the text file into its binary form. Moreover, this process of conversion is referred to as compilation.

Most programming languages like C, Java, C++ and Pascal, besides many others require compilation and you will need to install their respective compilers before you can execute any programs written using them.

Interpreter

Unlike the programming languages mentioned above, there are some other programming languages like Python and Perl that do not require compiler. Therefore, instead of a compiler, they need an interpreter, which is also software. The interpreter simply reads the program from the text file and as it parses the file, it converts the contents of the file and executes them. If you are working on any such programming languages, remember to install the corresponding interpreter on your system before starting.

If you haven't worked with a computer before or have little to no experience in installing software on the computer, technical advice from an expert is recommended. However, be sure to do the installation yourself, as it will help you build an acquaintance with the device that you will work with in the near future.

Besides this, if your computer does not support installation of any of the programming environment elements, you can also make use of the online compilers and interpreters that are available for all the different programming languages nowadays. All you need is a good Internet connection and a web browser to open these online facilities and get started with your programming lessons and practice sessions right away.

Chapter 2: Data Analysis with Python

Another topic that we need to explore a bit here is how Python, and some of the libraries that come with it, can work with the process of data analysis. This is an important process for any businesses because it allows them to take all of the data and information they have been collecting for a long time, and then can put it to good use once they understand what has been said within the information. It can be hard for a person to go through all of this information and figure out what is there, but for a data analyst who is able to use Python to complete the process, it is easy to find the information and the trends that you need.

The first thing that we need to look at here though is what data analysis is all about. Data analysis is going to be the process that companies can use in order to extract out useful, relevant, and even meaningful information from the data they collect, in a manner that is systematic. This ensures that they are able to get the full information out of everything and see some great results in the process. There are a number of reasons that a company would choose to work on their own data analysis, and this can include:

1. Parameter estimation, which helps them to infer some of the unknowns that they are dealing with.
2. Model development and prediction. This is going to be a lot of forecasting in the mix.
3. Feature extraction which means that we are going to identify some of the patterns that are there.
4. Hypothesis testing. This is going to allow us to verify the information and trends that we have found.
5. Fault detection. This is going to be the monitoring of the process that you are working on to make sure that there aren't any biases that happen in the information.

One thing that we need to make sure that we are watching out for is the idea of bias in the information that we have. If you go into the data analysis with the idea that something should turn out a certain way, or that you are going to manipulate the data so it fits the ideas that you have, there are going to be some problems. You can always change the data to say what you would like, but this doesn't mean that you are getting the true trends that come with this information, and you may be missing out on some of the things that you actually need to know about.

This is why a lot of data analysts will start this without any kind of hypothesis at all. This allows them to see the actual trends that come with this, and then see where the information is going to take you, without any kind of slant with the information that you have. This can make life easier and ensures that you are actually able to see what is truly in the information, rather than what you would like to see in that information.

Now, there are going to be a few different types of data that you can work with. First, there is going to be the deterministic. This is going to also be known as the data analysis that is non-random. And then there is going to be the stochastic, which is pretty much any kind that is not going to fit into the category of deterministic.

The Data Life Cycle

As we go through this information, it is important to understand some of the different phases that come with the data life cycle. Each of these comes together to ensure that we are able to understand the information that is presented to us and that we are able to use all of the data in the most efficient and best way possible.

There are a few stages that are going to come with this data life cycle, and we are going to start out with some of the basics to discuss each one to help us see what we are able to do with the data available to us. First, we work with data capture. The first experience that an individual or a company should have with a data item is to have it pass through the firewalls of the enterprise. This is going to be known as the Data Capture, which is basically going to be the act of creating values of data that do not exist yet and have never actually existed in that enterprise either. There are three ways that you can capture the data including:

1. Data acquisition: This is going to be the ingestion of data that is already existing that was produced by the organization but outside of the chosen enterprise.
2. Data entry: This is when we are dealing with the creation of new data values to help with the enterprise and it is done by devices or human operators that can help to generate the data needed.
3. Signal reception: This is where we are going to capture the data that a device has created with us, typically in the control system, but can be found in the Internet of Things if we would like.

The next part is going to be known as Data Maintenance. This is going to be where you supply the data to points at which data synthesis and data usage can occur in the next few steps. And it is best if you are able to work out the points so that they are going to be ready to go in this kind of phase.

What we will see during the data maintenance is that we are working to process the data, without really working to derive any value out of it yet. This is going to include integration changed data, cleansing, and making sure that the data is in the right format and as complete as possible before we get started. This ensures that no matter what method or algorithm you choose to work with here, you are going to be able to have the data ready to go.

Once you have been able to maintain the data and get it all cleaned up, it is time to work on the part known as data synthesis. This is a newer phase in the cycle and there are some places where you may not see this happen. This is going to be where we create some of the values of data through inductive logic, and using some of the data that we have from somewhere else as the input. The data synthesis is going to be the arena of analytics that is going to use modeling of some kind to help you get the right results in the end.

Data usage comes next. This data usage is going to be the part of the process where we are going to apply the data as information to tasks that the enterprise needs to run and then handle the management on its own. This would be a task that normally falls outside of your life cycle for the data. However, data is becoming such a central part of the model for most businesses and having this part done can make a big difference.

For example, the data itself can be a service or a product, or at least part of this service or product. This would then make it a part of the data usage as well. The usage of the data is going to have some special challenges when it comes to data governance. One of these is whether it is legal to use the data in the ways that most people in business would like. There could be some issues like contractual or regulatory constraints on how we can use this data and it is important that these are maintained as much as possible.

Once we have figured out the data usage, it is time to move on to data publication. In being used, it may be possible that our single data value may be sent outside of the enterprise. This is going to be known as the data publication, which we can define as the sending of data to a location that is not within the enterprise.

A good example of this would be when you have a brokerage that sends out some monthly statements to their client. Once the data has been sent outside the enterprise, it is de facto impossible to get that information back. When the values of data are wrong and you publish it, it is impossible to correct them because they are now beyond the reach of your enterprise. The idea of Data Governance, like we talked about before, is going to have to handle how this information that is incorrect can be handled with.

Next on the list is the data archival. We will see that the single data value that we are working with can sometimes experience a lot of different rounds of usage and then publication, but eventually, it is going to reach the very end of its life. The first part of this means that we need to be able to take the value of the data and archive it. When we work on the process of Data Archival, it is going to mean that we are copying the data to an environment where it is stored in case we need it again, in an active production environment, and then we will remove the data from all of those active environments as well.

This kind of archive for the data is simply going to be a place where the data is stored, but where no publication, usage, or maintenance is going to happen. If necessary, it is possible to take any of the data that is in the archive and bring it back out to use again.

And finally, we reach the part of data purging. This is going to be the end that comes with our single data value and the life cycle that it has gone through. Data purging is going to be when we remove every copy of data from the enterprise. If possible, you will reach this information through the archive. If there is a challenge from Data Governance at this point, it is just there to prove that the information and the data have gone through the proper purging procedure at that time.

-

Working with data analysis and why it is important

With this in mind, we need to pay attention to why we would want to work on data analysis to start with? Do we really need to be able to look through all of this information to find the trends, or is there another method? Let's look at an example of what can happen when we do this data analysis and why you would want to use it.

Let's consider that we are looking at a set of data that includes information about the weather that occurred across the globe between the years 2015 to 2018. We are also going to have information that is base don the country between these years as well. So, there is going to be a percentage of ran within that country and we are going to have some data that concerns this in our set of data as well.

Now, what if you would like to go through all of that data, but you would like to only take a look at the data that comes with one specific country. Let's say that you would like to look at America and you want to see what percentage of rain it received between 2016 and 2017. Now, how are you going to get this information in a quick and efficient manner?

What we would need to do to make sure that we were able to get ahold of this particular set of data is to work with the data analysis. There are several algorithms, especially those that come from machine learning, that would help you to figure out the percentage of rain that America gets between 2016 to 2017. And this whole process is going to be known as what data analysis is really all about.

The Python Panda Library

When it comes to doing some data analysis in Python, the best extension that you can use is Pandas. This is an open-sourced library that works well with Python and it is going to provide you with a high level of performance, data structures that are easy for even a beginner to use, and tools to make data analysis easy with Python. There are a lot of things to enjoy about this language, and if you want to be able to sort through all of the great information that you have available with the help of Python, then this is the library that you need to work with.

There are a lot of things that you can enjoy when it comes to working on the Python library. First off, this is one of the most popular and easy to use libraries when it comes to data science and it is going to work on top of the NumPy library. The name of Pandas that was given to this library is derived from the word of Panel Data, which is going to be an Econometrics from Multidimensional data. And one thing that a lot of coders are going to like about working with Pandas is that it is able to take a lot of the data that you need, including a SQL database or a TSV and CSV file, and will use it to create an object in Python. This object is going to have columns as well as rows called the data frame, something that looks very similar to what we see with a table in statistical software including Excel.

There are many different features that are going to set Pandas apart from some of the other libraries that are out there. Some of the benefits that you are going to enjoy the most will include:

1. There are some data frames or data structures that are going to be high level compared to some of the others that you can use.
2. There is going to be a streamlined process in place to handle the tabular data, and then

there is also a functionality that is rich for the time series that you want to work with.

3. There is going to be the benefit of data alignment, missing data-friendly statistics, merge, join, and groupby methods to help you handle the data that you have.

4. You are able to use the variety of structures for data in Pandas, and you will be able to freely draw on the functions that are present in SciPy and NumPy to help make sure manipulation and other work can be done the way that you want.

Before we move on from here, we also need to have a good look at what some of the types of data are when it comes to Pandas. Pandas is going to be well suited when it comes to a large amount of data and will be able to help you sort through almost any kind of data that you would like. Some of the data types that are going to be the most suitable for working with the Pandas library with Python will include:

1. Any kind of tabular data that is going to have columns that are heterogeneously typed.

2. Arbitrary matrix data that has labels for the columns and rows.
3. Unordered and ordered time-series data
4. Any other kinds of sets of data that are statistical and observational.

Working with the Pandas library is one of the best ways to handle some of the Python codings that you want to do with the help of data analysis. As a company, it is so important to be able to go through and not just collect data, but also to be able to read through that information and learn some of the trends and the information that is available there. being able to do this can provide your company with some of the insights that it needs to do better, and really grow while providing customer service.

There are a lot of different methods that you can use when it comes to performing data analysis. And some of them are going to work in a different way than we may see with Python or with the Pandas library. But when it comes to efficiently and quickly working through a lot of data, and having a multitude of algorithms and more that can sort through all of this information, working with the Python Pandas is the best option.

Chapter 3: Fundamentals of Statistics

Why Statistics is Important for Data Science?

Some of the algorithms in machine learning have been borrowed from statistics. So, we need some basic knowledge of statistics to understand how to extract useful information from data and how to build estimation models for data prediction based on hypothesis and assumptions. For example, linear regression is widely used in several machine learning problems. In statistics, it is used for fitting a line to data values while in machine learning, it is more like learning weights (constant values in line equation) through examples.

Some uses of statistics in machine learning are:

• Data Understanding: *Understanding distribution of data variables and their relationships. So, we can design a model predictor best suited for data. For this, we need to understand what data distribution is, what* relationships our variables can have and how to understand those relationships.

• Data Cleaning: *We cannot simply get raw data and feed it to machine learning models for our task. There are certain complexities within. For example, the data might be corrupted, erroneous or just missing. So, we need to fix those issues e.g. we can fill the missing data following the same data distribution, we can identify outliers and abnormal data distributions to eliminate corruption or errors.*

• *Data Preparation*: Sometimes, our data features are not all on the same scale which leads to some issues in model training (It is further explained in training models part). Sometimes, the data is textual and we need to encode it in numeric form to make it compatible for our model. So we need data scaling, sampling and encoding from statistics.

• Model Configuration and Selection: *Hyperparameters of a machine learning model control the learning method which can lead to different results from the model. Using statistical hypothesis testing technique from statistics, we can compare results of different hyperparameters. Similarly, we need such statistical techniques to select a model by comparing models' results and their properties.*

• Model Evaluation: *To evaluate a model, we need statistical methods for data sampling and resampling. We also need metrics to properly evaluate model and quantify the variability in predictions using estimation statistics.*

Data Types

Data in statistics is classified in following types and subtypes:

1. Qualitative Data
   1. Nominal/Categorical
   2. Ordinal
2. Quantitative Data
   1. Discrete

2. Continuous

    1.   Interval

    2.   Ratio

Qualitative Data

Qualitative data is non-numerical and categorical data. Categorical data can be counted, grouped and ranked in order of importance. Such data is grouped to bring order or make sense of the data.

Nominal:

Nominal scales represent data that does not have quantitative values or any numerical significance. This scale is used for classification or categorization of the variables. These variables are simply labels of data without any specific order. Such scale is often used in surveys and questionnaires.

Of these three colors, which one do you like the most?

    1.   Red

    2.   Green

    3.   Blue

For example, in the above question, color is a categorical variable but there is no specific way to order these colors from low to high or high to low.

So, for a question in a survey:

Which pizza crust do you like?

1. Thin Crust
2. Stuffed Crust
3. Cheese Stuffed Crust
4. Hand Tossed Crust

Only the types of crust are significant of analysis and their order does not matter. The results of such questions are analyzed to provide the most common answer which describes the customers' preferences.

ORDINAL:

Ordinal scale represents data that has some specific order. That order relates elements of data to each other in a ranked fashion. Numbers can be assigned as labels and are not mathematically measured as scales.

How satisfied you are with your test scores:

1. Extremely Unsatisfied
2. Unsatisfied
3. Neutral
4. Satisfied
5. Extremely Satisfied

Here, these options are assigned numbers, that is, a ranking of 5 is better than a ranking of 3 but we cannot quantify the difference between these two rankings (i.e. how good ranking 5 is compared to ranking 3).

Quantitative Data

Data that is numerical or can be measured is called quantitative data. For example, heights of 12 years old boys, GPA of a class, Distance of stars, Temperature of the day and so on. Numerical data have two sub data types:

1. Discrete
2. Continuous

DISCRETE:

Discrete data is numerical data that can not be subdivided into smaller parts. For example, number of people in a room, number of apples in a basket, number of planets in solar system, etc.

CONTINUOUS:

Continuous data can be broken down into smaller parts. For example, temperature, distance, weight of a person, etc. Continuous data can be further categorized into two types:

1. Interval
2. Ratio

Interval:

Interval scale represents data that has specific order and that order has mathematical significance, which means that unlike nominal and ordinal scales, the interval scale quantifies the difference between the order of variables. This scale is quite effective because we can apply statistical analysis on such data. The only drawback of this scale is that we cannot compute ratios because it does not have a true zero value (a starting point for values) and hence, a zero value does not mean "absence of value" and is therefore not meaningful.

For example, 70 degree Celcius is less than 90 degree Celcius and their difference is a measurable 20 C as is the difference between 90 C and 110 C. Also, 40 degree Celcius is not twice as hot as 20 degree Celcius. A value of 0 C is arbitrary as it does not mean "no temperature" and because negative values of temperature do exist.

Ratio:

Ratio scale has all the properties from Interval scale and also defines a true zero value. A meaningful zero in ratio scale means "absence of value". Because of the existence of a true zero value, variables of ratio scale does not have negative values and it allows to measure ratio between two variables. This scale allows to apply techniques of inferential and descriptive statistics to variables. Some examples of ratio variables are height, weight, money, age and time.

For example, what is your weight in pounds?

- *< 100 lbs*

- *100 lbs - 120 lbs*

- *121 lbs - 140 lbs*

- *141 lbs - 160 lbs*

- *> 160 lbs*

Similarly, there is no such thing as age 0, because that essentially means you don't exist. Because of this, we can compare that an age of 24 is twice the age of 12 and that we cannot have negative age value.

Statistics in Practice

Statistics is defined as the collection, analysis and interpretation of data. It transforms raw data to useful information and helps us understand our data required to train our machine learning models and interpret their results. The field of statistics has two major divisions: Descriptive statistics and Inferential statistics. Both of these divisions combined are powerful tools for data understanding, description and data prediction. Descriptive statistics describes and interprets data and helps us understand how two variables or processes are related while inferential statistics is used to reason from available data.

Descriptive Statistics

Descriptive statistics describes features of data by summarizing it. For example we have test scores of 100 students from a class. Descriptive statistics gives detailed information about those scores e.g. how spread the scores are, if there are outliers (scores way above or lower than average score), how scores are distributed (how many students with low score, high score or average score) and many other similar stats of those results.

Basic Definitions

POPULATION

Population is something under observation for study. It is a set of observations. It also describes the subject of a particular study. For example, if we are studying weights of men, the population would be the set of weights of all men of the world.

Population Parameters

Population parameters are characteristics and stats about population such as mean, standard deviation.

Sample

Sample is a randomly taken small part of the population or just a subset of the population. The observations and conclusions made on sample data represent properties or attributes of the entire population. For example, consider a study where we want to know how many hours, on average, do a teenager spends in physical exercise. Since, surveying all the teenagers of the world or even a country is impractical because of time and resource constraint. So, we take a sample from the population that represents the entire population.

Descriptive statistics is further divided into measures of center and measures of dispersion.

1. Measures of Center
   1. Mean
   2. Median
   3. Mode
2. Measures of Dispersion
   1. Range
   2. Percentiles/Quartiles
   3. Interquartile range
   4. Variance
   5. Standard Deviation
   6. Kurtosis
   7. Skewness

Measure of Center/Central Tendency

Central tendency describes a dataset with a single value which is the central position within that dataset. This central position provides summary of the whole data.

Three measures of central tendency are:

- Mean

- Median

- Mode

Mean

It refers to the mean or average of data and is the sum of all values of the data divided by the number of values. It is represented by letter μ or x and is given by:

$$\mu = \frac{1}{n}\sum_{i=1}^{n} x_i$$

Some properties of mean make it very useful for measuring

For example, consider following array of numbers and their mean calculated:

Given Array: $\{-5, 6, 3, 0, 6\}$

$$\mu = \frac{(-5 + 6 + 3 + 0 + 6)}{5} = \frac{10}{5}$$

$\mu = 2.0$

A disadvantage of using statistical mean is that it can be biased because it is affected by outliers in the data. Consider the above example again and see how the existence of an outlier will affect the mean value:

Given Array: $\{-5, 6, 3, 0, 6, 110\}$

$$\mu = \frac{(-5 + 6 + 3 + 0 + 6 + 110)}{6} = \frac{120}{6}$$

$\mu = 20.0$

Median

Median is another measure of central tendency and is the middle value of ascendingly sorted data. If the number of values in dataset is even, the median is the mean value of two middle values in sorted array.

Given Array { − 5, 6, 3, 0, 6 }

Sorted in Ascending Order { − 5, 0, 3, 6, 6 }

Median is our middle value in sorted array = 3

One important property of median is that it is not affected by outliers. Consider the example of statistical mean with outlier:

Given Array { − 5, 6, 3, 0, 6, 110 }

Sorted in Ascending Order { − 5, 0, 3, 6, 6, 110 }

$$Median = \frac{(3 + 6)}{2} = \frac{9}{2}$$

Median = 4.5

So, median should be used when data is skewed (not symmetric).

Mode

Mode is the most frequently occurring value in the data. Some datasets can be multimodal (having more than one modes) and some may not have any mode at all. For example,

Given Array $\{1, 6, 0, 9, 3, -2, 4, -1, -1, 5, 1, 5, 3, 1, 7, -3, -4, 7, 8, -1\}$

Modes: $-1, 1$

Given Array: $\{-1, 7, 3, 15, 2\}$

This data does not have any mode

Mode is rarely used as central measure of tendency. One problem with mode is that there can be multiple modes in data and they can be spread out.

Following three histograms with different symmetric and skewed distributions show three measures of center. In case of symmetric (normal) distribution, mean, median and mode are all same. Although we can use any of these three measures but mean is usually preferred because it considers all the values of data in calculation, which is not the case for median and mode.

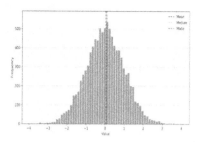

Now consider when the data is right skewed. Here, mean is not a good representation of the center of dataset and so, we can better choose median measure.

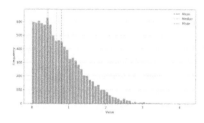

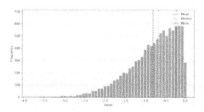

Measures of Dispersion

Measure of dispersion tells how much the data distribution is stretched out or how variable the data is. Sometimes, measure of central tendency is not enough to grasp the distribution of data. For example, two data distributions can have same mean but one distribution can be more spread out than the other.

Range

It is the simplest measure of dispersion. It is the difference between the maximum value and the minimum value of the data.

Given Array: $\{-4, 7, 1, 7, -5, 6, 3, 0\}$

Range: $7 - (-5) = 12$

Range provides us a quick way to get a rough idea of the spread of distribution but it does not give much detail about the data. Two datasets can have same range but their values can vary significantly. Also, range is sensitive to outliers or extreme values.

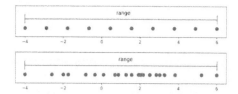

Percentile

A percentile represents a value below which a given percentage of data falls. In other words, percentile is the relative position of a value in sorted dataset. A student scored 89 out of 100 in a test. This figure alone does not have significant meaning unless we know what was his/her position in class. May be, a score of 89 falls in the 30th percentile which means that it is better than 30% of the class or may be 70th percentile (70% of students have scored less than 89 on test).

Index of a number at Pth percentile in an ordered list of values is given by:

$$Index = \frac{P}{100} * N$$

For example,

Given Sorted Values: { − 1,5,12,13,30,50}

For example, for list of numbers given above,

$15th\ percentile : P_{15}$
$$= \frac{15}{100} * 6 = 0.9 \approx 1\ (1st\ number\ in\ the\ list$$
$)$

$30th\ percentile : P_{30}$
$$= \frac{30}{100} * 6 = 1.8 \approx 2\ (2nd\ number\ in\ the\ list$$
$)$

$60th\ percentile : P_{60}$
$$= \frac{60}{100} * 6 = 3.6 \approx 4\ (4th\ number\ in\ the\ list$$
$)$

$99th\ percentile : P_{99}$
$$= \frac{99}{100} * 6 = 5.9 \approx 6\ (6th\ number\ in\ the\ list$$
$)$

Quartiles

Quartiles are three values that divide a dataset into 4 parts where each part contains 25% of the total data. First, second and third quartiles are actually 25th, 50th and 75th percentiles respectively. First quartile divides the data in 1:3 parts and has 25% of data on the left side(or below it). Second quartile divides the data in 1:1 while the third quartile divides the data in 3:1 parts (75% data on left side). So, second quartile is actually the middle value (or median) of the dataset and it divides the data into two equal parts. Then, first quartile is the middle value (or median) of the first part and third quartile is the middle value (or median) of the second part.

For example,

Given array:

[10, − 9, − 7, 10, 3, − 10, − 2, − 3, 14, − 2, − 6, − 9, 14, 16, 0]

Sorted array:

$$[-10, -9, -9, -7, -6, -3, -2,$$
$$-2, 0, 3, 10, 10, 14, 14, 16]$$

$Q_1 = -2$

InterQuartile Range

Interquartile range (IRQ) is the difference between third quartile and first quartile. An important property of IQR is that it is not affected by outlier values, which makes it preferable over range. It focuses on the middle 50% values of data.

Sorted array:

$[-10, -9, -9, -7, -6, -3, -2, -2, 0, 3, 10, 10, 14, 14, 16]$

$IRQ: 16.5$

Visual representation of some of these measures is shown in following boxplot.

Variance

It is a measure of the spread of data. It quantifies how far, on average, the data is from the mean value.

$$Var(X) = \frac{1}{N}\sum_{i=1}^{N}(x_i - \mu)^2$$

Standard Deviation

Standard deviation is just the square root of variance. The difference between variance and standard deviation is that variance value is on a large scale while standard deviation has the same scale as other dataset values. It is represented by the greek letter σ and is given by:

$$\sigma = \sqrt{Var(X)}$$

For example, consider following values, their mean and standard deviation has been calculated:

{2, 8, 0, 2, − 2, − 4, 7, 1, 7, − 5, 6, 3, 0, 6, 8, 6, 2, 6, − 3, 9}

$\mu = 2.95$

$\sigma = 4.2$

Skewness

Skewness is a measure of data asymmetry. A symmetric distribution means that the data values are equally distributed around the mean value, as in the case of a normal distribution. In case of asymmetry, data is distributed unevenly or the distribution is not symmetrical about the mean. In positively skewed data

50

distribution, values are concentrated to the left and in negatively skewed data, values are concentrated to the right as shown in figure below. If data skewness is not close to zero, the data is not normally distributed.

$$Skewness = \frac{\frac{1}{N}\sum_{i=1}^{N}(x_i - \mu)^3}{\sigma^3}$$

Kurtosis

Kurtosis describes the tail of a distribution with reference to a normal distribution. A normal distribution has a kurtosis equal to 3 and is called mesokurtic. A distribution with shorter and thinner tails, broader and lower peaks than a normal distribution is called platykurtic and has kurtosis less than 3. A distribution with longer tails, higher and sharper peaks than a normal distribution is called leptykurtic and has kurtosis greater than 3.

$$Kurtosis = \frac{\frac{1}{N}\sum_{i=1}^{N}(x_i - \mu)^4}{\sigma^4}$$

Where N is the number of values, μ is mean of values and σ is standard deviation.

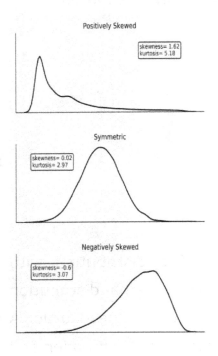

Chapter 4: Visualization and results

In the previous chapters we learnt how to handle data. In this chapter we are going to learn methods of visualizing data as well as creating figures to present analysis of data. In order to develop figures, many libraries are available in Python. This section presents only functionalities of the matplolib library which is an advanced library in Python to develop figures.

Matplotlib library in Python

Matplolib library is an open source advanced package available in Python for data visualization. Data visualization is crucial in data analysis as well as to communicate the results to stakeholders. This library is based on the NumPy library too. One module of matplotlib library that is very used is the Pyplot. This module has similar interface as Matlab a programming tool that is efficient for numerical programming. If you did not install matplotlib yet, you can do so by typing the following command in python prompt:

pip install matplotlib

If you have installed Anaconda and you are using Jupyter, this library should be already installed by default. All you have to do is import the package.

Before dining into examples and how to use the matplotlib library, let's see the component of a figure that we can set. A figure is entire figure that is formed by one or more axes which are called a plot. Axes is what is commonly named as a plot. A figure can be formed by different axes depending on the type of plotting we are making 1D, 2D or 3D. Axis are responsible of setting the limits of a plot. Artist is all the components that can be in a figure like a text object, collection objects.

Basic plot in matplotlib

We will start first in this chapter by the Pyplot module in matplotlib. This module offers the basic functions to supplement components to the current axes of a figure. To use this module, it should be imported as follows:

>>> import numpy as np

>>> import matplotlib.pyplot as plt

Note here we imported the Numpy library as well because we will be working with numpy arrays.

Now we can create a single plot of a data using the function plot(). Let's create a series of data and plot these data.

```
>>> X = np.array([1,2,3,4])

>>> Y = X ** 2

>>> plt.plot(X,Y)

>>> plt.show()
```

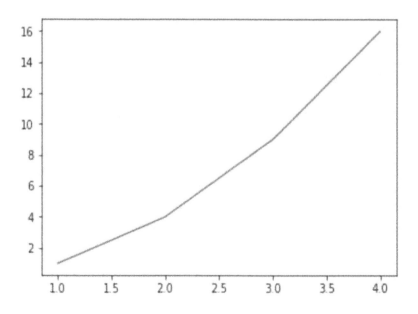

In this example, we created an array of values and computed the square of each value. The plot function is supplied with 2 inputs where the 1st argument is values of X-axis and the 2nd argument is corresponding values of Y-axis. Now it would be helpful to understand the plotting if we had a legend of the axis and a title for the plot. To add these elements into our plotting, we can use the *xlabel()* function that adds a label to the x-axis and *ylabel()* function that adds a label to the y-axis. The *title()* function adds a title to the plot.

```
>>> A = np.array([1,2,3,4])

>>> B = A ** 2

>>> plt.plot(A,B)

>>> plt.xlabel('A labels')

>>> plt.ylabel('B= A**2')

>>> plt.title('My first in Python')

>>> plt.show()
```

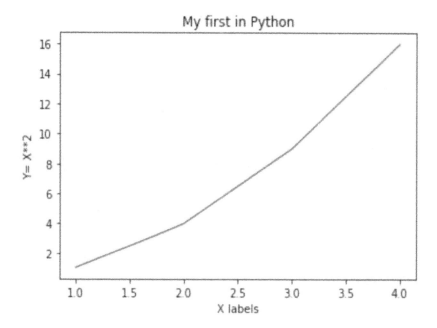

My first in Python

Now we can change the size of the figure using the figure function and passing argument that specifies the size of the figure. For example, let's change the size of the previous figure we created.

```
>>> A = np.array([1,2,3,4])

>>> B = A ** 2

>>> plt.figure(figsize=(5,5))

>>> plt.plot(A,B)

>>> plt.xlabel('A labels')

>>> plt.ylabel('B= A**2')
```

```
>>> plt.title('My first in Python with different size')

>>> plt.show()
```

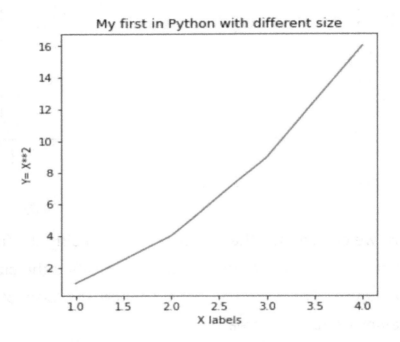

The plot function can take other input argument. In fact, we can plot two different datasets in the same plot. Let's define compute the values of X ** 3 and plot it in the same figure as an example.

```
>>> A = np.array([1,2,3,4])

>>> B = A ** 2
```

```
>>> B2 = A ** 3

    >>> plt.figure(figsize=(10,5))

    >>> plt.plot(A,B, A,B2)

    >>> plt.xlabel('A labels')

    >>> plt.ylabel('B= A**2')

        >>> plt.title('My first in Python with two
dataset')

    >>> plt.show()
```

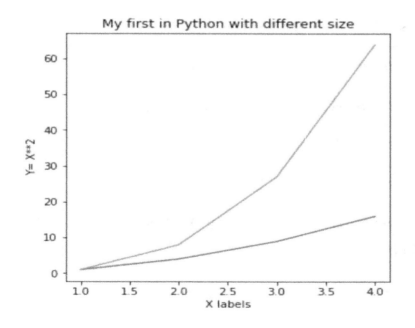

Note that by default the plot function used a different color to plot the second dataset. Also, by default plot function draws the data as a line. In fact, we can pass another argument to the plot function that will specify how the data is plot. In other words, we specify if data is plotted as a line or using another marker such '+', '*', '0'. We can also specify the color. For instance, 'go' will make the plot function to use o to plot the data and the data will be plotted in green. We can also specify the line width if the data is plotted as a line. For example:

```
>>> A = np.array([1,2,3,4])

>>> B=A ** 2

>>> B2 = A ** 3

>>> plt.figure(figsize=(10,5))

>>> plt.plot(A,B,A,B2,linewidth=5)

>>> plt.xlabel('A labels')

>>> plt.ylabel('B= A**2')

>>> plt.title('My first in Python with two datasets and Line width=5')

>>> plt.show()
```

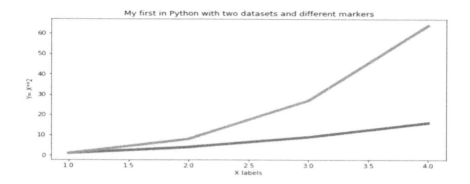

The following example uses different markers to plot two datasets:

```
>>> X = np.array([1,2,3,4])

>>> Y = X ** 2

>>> Y2 = X ** 3

>>> plt.figure(figsize=(5,5))

>>> plt.plot(X,Y,'r*', X,Y2, 'ko')

>>> plt.xlabel('X labels')

>>> plt.ylabel('Y= X**2')

>>> plt.title('My first in Python with two datasets
and different markers')

>>> plt.show()
```

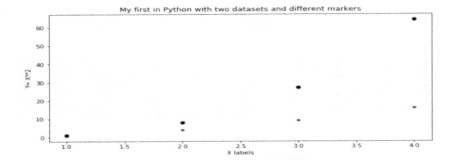

Multiple plots in same figure

You plot several plots in the same figure using the *subplot()* function. Note the datasets that we plotted in the previous section in the same plot can be plotted in different plots in the same figure. The *subplot()* function takes as inputs the following arguments ncols, nrows and finally index. The ncols indicate the number of columns in the figure, nrows the numbers of rows in the figure and the index point toward which plot. For example, we can plot our two datasets in a figure with two rows as follows:

>>> X = np.array([1,2,3,4])

>>> Y = X ** 2

>>> Y2 = X ** 3

>>> plt.figure(figsize=(10,10))

>>> plt.subplot(2,1,1)

```
>>> plt.plot(X,Y,linewidth=5)

>>> plt.xlabel('X labels')

>>> plt.ylabel('Y= X**2')

>>> plt.title('My first subplot in Python')

>>> plt.subplot(2,1,2)

>>> plt.plot(X,Y2,linewidth=5)

>>> plt.xlabel('X labels')

>>> plt.ylabel('Y= X**3')

>>> plt.title('My second subplot in Python')

>>> plt.show()
```

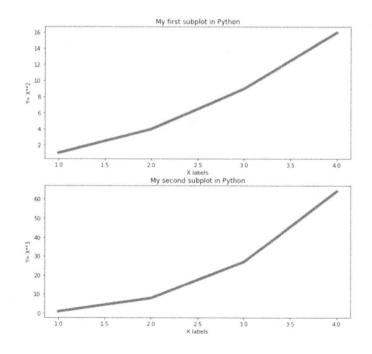

We can plot the two data set in a figure with two columns and two rows by passing as argument to the subplot (1,2,1) and (1,2,2) as follows:

```
>>> X = np.array([1,2,3,4])
>>> Y = X ** 2
>>> Y2 = X ** 3
>>> plt.figure(figsize=(10,10))
>>> plt.subplot(1,2,1)
>>> plt.plot(X,Y,linewidth=5)
>>> plt.xlabel('X labels')
>>> plt.ylabel('Y= X**2')
>>> plt.title('My first subplot in Python')
>>> plt.subplot(1,2,2)
>>> plt.plot(X,Y2,linewidth=5)
>>> plt.xlabel('X labels')
>>> plt.ylabel('Y= X**3')
>>> plt.title('My second subplot in Python')
>>> plt.show()
```

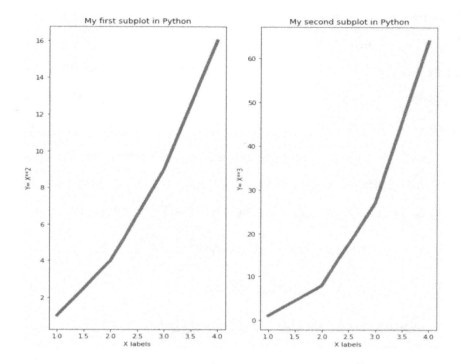

Type of plots

The matplotlib offers several functions to create different graphs that are useful in data science and statistical analysis. The bar graphs are a handy graph to assess and compare different groups among data and explore their distribution. The *bar()* function take as input argument a set of categorial data and their associated values. It takes also optionally a color if you want to make a bar graph where each category is represented with a specific color. For example, let's take the Iris data from the example in the previous chapter about Data frame data structure. Remember the Iris data is formed by a by a sample of 3 species of the Iris flower. Each species is described by sepals and petals length and sepals and petals width. This dataset is available in the sklearn library from which we are going to import the dataset. Because we will be using DataFrame structure we will import the Pandas library as well and we are going to create a Dataframe for the Iris dataset.

```
>>> import pandas as pd

>>> import numpy as np

>>> from sklearn import datasets

>>> Iris = datasets.load_iris()

I>>> Iris_d = Iris.data

>>>    Iris_DF    =    pd.DataFrame(Iris_d,
columns=Iris.feature_names)
```

The Iris data set has also a variable associated with each value of the sepal length and width as well as lengths and width of the petal. This variable indicates the Iris follower's species and is stored in the variable target. In the following command we are going to create a variable for this variable target:

<u>>>> Y = Iris.target</u>

Now that we have our data ready, we are going to plot a bar graph of the sepal length as follows:

>>> plt.bar(Y, Iris_DF['sepal length (cm)'])

>>> plt.title(' Bar Graph of the Sepal length')

>>> plt.xlabel(' Iris Species')

>>> plt.ylabel(' Count')

>>> plt.show()

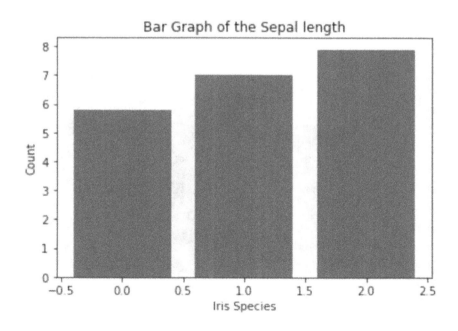

By default, Python plot figures in blue. We can change the color of the bars in the graph by passing the argument color as follows:

>>> plt.bar(Y, Iris_DF['sepal length (cm)'], color='black')

>>> plt.title(' Bar Graph of the Sepal length')

>>> plt.xlabel(' Iris Species')

>>> plt.ylabel(' Count')

>>> plt.show()

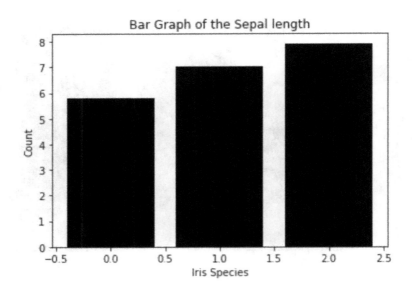

We can also change the orientation of the bars from vertical bars to horizontal bars using the function *barh()*. The barh() function takes the same input argument as the *bar()* function. Let's plot horizontal bar graph for the sepal width length for each Iris species.

>>> plt.barh(Y,Iris_DF['sepal length (cm)'], color='black')

>>> plt.title(' Bar Graph of the Sepal length')

>>> plt.xlabel(' Iris Species')

>>> plt.ylabel(' Count')

>>> plt.show()

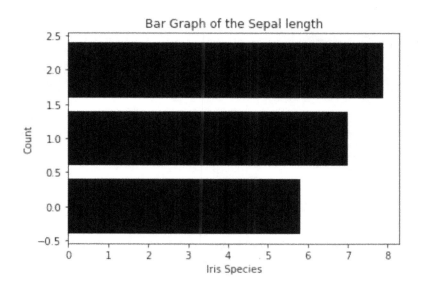

We can also supply the *bar()* or the *barh()* function with an extra argument xerr or yerr(if using the *bar()* function) and its values. For example, if we want o plot also the variance of the variable for which the bar graph is plotted. For example, in the case of the sepal length we can do if we are using *barh()* function:

>>> # Computing the variance with Numpy library

>>> V = np.var(Iris_DF['sepal length (cm)'])

>>> plt.barh(Y, Iris_DF['sepal length (cm)'], xerr = V, color = 'grey')

>>> plt.title(' Bar Graph of the Sepal length with Variance')

>>> plt.xlabel(' Iris Species')

>>> plt.ylabel(' Count')

>>> plt.show()

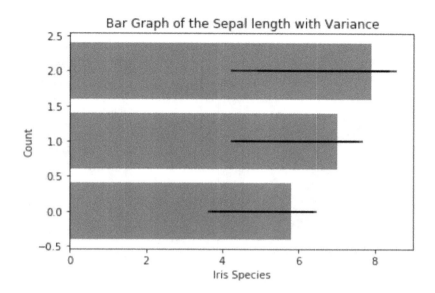

Bar Graph of the Sepal length with Variance

If the function *bar()* is used for vertical bars, to plot the variance with bars we pass as argument yerr as follows:

>>> plt.bar(Y, Iris_DF['sepal length (cm)'], yerr = V, color = 'grey')

>>> plt.title(' Bar Graph of the Sepal length with Variance')

>>> plt.xlabel(' Iris Species')

>>> plt.ylabel(' Count')

>>> plt.show()

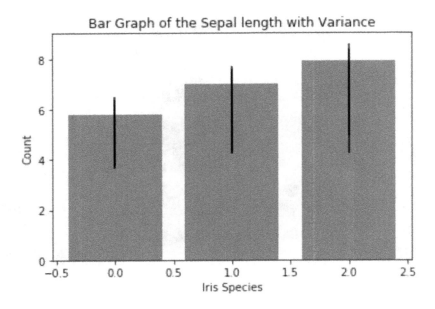

Sometimes, we have a dataset with multiple variables and we want to create a single bar graph that shows the bars for different variables for each category like in the case of the Iris data set we are using in this chapter. To plot or stack multiple bars in the same graph, we need to use the *bar()* function as many times as the number of the variables for which the graph are plotted. In this case, we need to specify the index and width for the bars to stack them together. Let's see how we can use this in order to plot in the same graph sepal length and sepal width bars. First, we need to group the Iris flowers according to the species and compute the mean sepal length and mean sepal width for each species.

Remember we can do that using the *groupby()* function like we did in the previous chapter. We also need to add the Y variable which indicates the Iris species into our DataFrame.

```
>>> data = Iris_DF
```

```
>>> data['Y'] = Y # Adding the Y variable to the Dataframe
```

>>> grouped_data = data.groupby(' Y ') # Grouping the Iris flowers according to the species

>>> # Computing the mean sepal length and width for each species

```
>>> M = grouped_data['sepal length (cm)'].agg(np.mean)
```

```
>>> M2 = grouped_data['sepal width (cm)'].agg(np.mean)
```

```
>>> print(' The mean sepal length (cm) for each species is:', M)
```

```
The mean sepal length (cm) for each species is:
Y
0   5.006
```

1   5.936

2   6.588

Name: sepal length (cm), dtype: float64

>>> print(' The mean width (cm) of the sepal for each species is:', M)

The mean sepal width (cm) for each species is: Y

0   5.006

1 5.936

2 6.588

Name: sepal length (cm), dtype: float64

Now that the data is ready, we plot the stacked bar graph as follows:

```
>>> ind = np.arange(3)
>>> width = 0.3
>>> plt.bar (ind, M, width, color = 'grey')
>>> plt.bar (ind + width, M2, width, color = 'blue')
```

```
>>> plt.title(' Bar Graph of the Sepal length and
width (cm)')

>>> plt.xlabel(' Iris Species')

>>> plt.ylabel(' Count')

>>> plt.show()
```

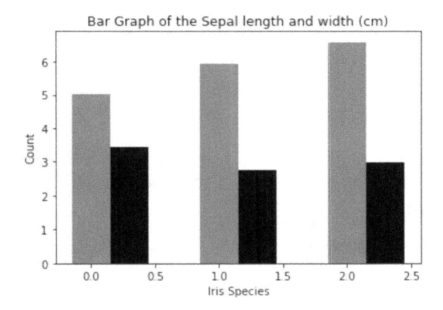

We can add a legend to our graph using the *legend()* function in oder to distinguish between the graphs. We can also define specify in the graph the position of ticks in axis. The following statements how we can do that:

```
>>> ind = np.arange(3)
```

```
>>> width = 0.3

>>> plt.bar (ind, M, width, color = 'grey', label =
'Sepal length(cm)')

>>> plt.bar (ind + width, M2, width, color =
'blue', label = 'Sepal width(cm)')

>>> plt.title(' Bar Graph of the Sepal length and
width (cm)')

>>> plt.xlabel(' Iris Species')

>>> plt.ylabel(' Count')

>>> plt.xticks(ind + width/2, ind) # Position of
the xticks

>>> plt.legend(loc = 'best') # Position of the
legend

>>> plt.show()
```

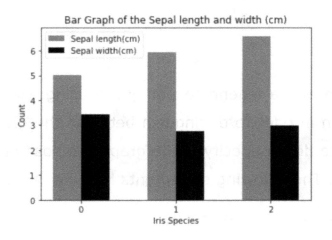

We can also stack the bars vertically. In this case we pass an argument to the *bar()* function fro the second variable and specify the bar graph of the values below. For example, to stack vertically the sepal lenght and width we follow the code presented in below:

```
>>> ind = np.arange(3)

>>> width = 0.3

>>> plt.bar (ind, M, width, color = 'grey', label = 'Sepal length(cm)')

>>> plt.bar (ind, M2, width, color = 'blue', label = 'Sepal width(cm)', bottom = M)

>>> plt.title(' Bar Graph of the Sepal length and width (cm)')

>>> plt.xlabel(' Iris Species')

>>> plt.ylabel(' Count')

>>> plt.xticks(ind + width/2, ind) # Position of the xticks

>>> plt.legend(loc = 'best') # Position of the legend

>>> plt.show()
```

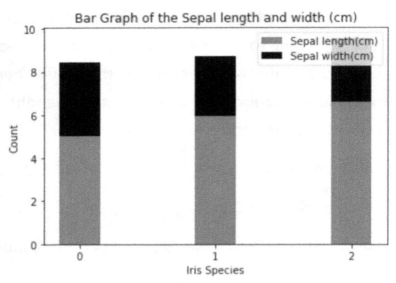

Bar Graph of the Sepal length and width (cm)

Histograms are another common graph in data analysis and statistical analysis that show the distribution of a variable. The histogram is a plot that shows the frequency of the values that a variable can take. In other words, we plot the range values of a variable against its frequency which describe the distribution of the variable. The *hist()* function allows to plot histograms with matplotlib library. For example, let's plot the histogram of the sepal length of the Iris data:

```
>>> plt.title(' Histogram of the Iris sepal length')

>>> plt.xlabel ('Sepal length (cm)')

>>> plt.ylabel (' Frequency')

>>> plt.hist(Iris_DF['sepal length (cm)'])
```

```
>>> plt.show()
```

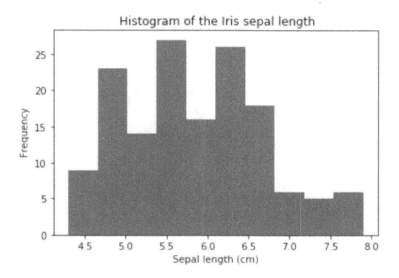

Like the other plot functions, color of the histogram can be changed by passing a color input argument like in the following example:

```
>>> plt.title(' Histogram of the Iris sepal length')

>>> plt.xlabel ('Sepal length (cm)')

>>> plt.ylabel (' Frequency')

>>> plt.hist(Iris_DF['sepal length (cm)'], color =
'grey')

>>> plt.show()
```

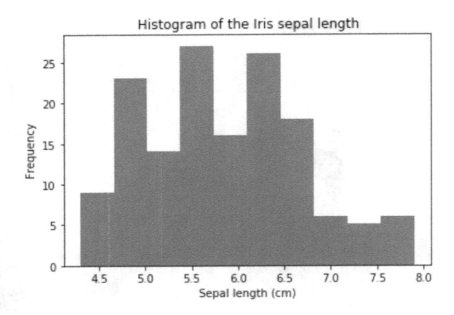

Histogram of the Iris sepal length

In order to detect visually correlation between the variables we can use scatter plots that plots variables against each other in 2-dimensional space. To plot a scatter plot, we use the function *scatter()*. For example, we plot the sepal length against the sepal width:

```
>>> plt.scatter(Iris_DF['sepal    length    (cm)'],
Iris_DF['sepal width (cm)'])
```

```
>>> plt.title( ' Scatter plot of sepal length and sepal width')
```

```
>>> plt.xlabel(' Sepal length (cm)')
```

```
>>> plt.ylabel (' Sepal width (cm)')
```

```
>>> plt.show()
```

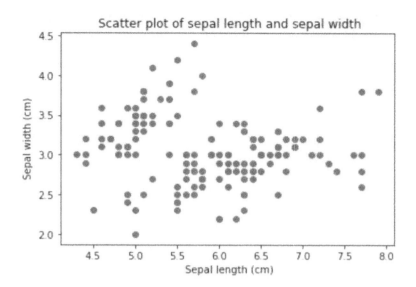

Scatter plot of sepal length and sepal width

The scatter plot in the figure above is in a 2-dimensional space. We can also visualize the same scatter in a 3-dimensional space using *scatter3D()* function. This function is part of the mplot3d for 3 dimensional plots. So, we import first the module than plot the scatter plot in a 3-dimensional plot as follows:

>>> from mpl_toolkits import mplot3d

>>> ax = plt.axes(projection='3d')

>>> **ax.scatter3D (Iris_DF['sepal length (cm)'], Iris_DF['sepal width (cm)'])**

>>> ax.set_xlabel(' Sepal length (cm)')

>>> ax.set_ylabel (' Sepal width (cm)')

>>> ax.set_title(' 3-D scatter plot of sepal length and sepal width')

>>> plt.show()

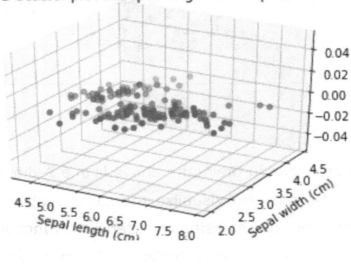

3-D scatter plot of sepal length and sepal width

Chapter 5: Writing Loops in Python

The next thing that we need to take a look at when it is time to write some of your own codes in Python will be looped. Creating loops can help you to make a code that is more efficient, and will ensure that you are able to get codes written quickly and without a ton of work in the process. These loops work well with some of the conditional statements that we are going to talk about, later on, helping you to clear up your code while getting a lot done in a short amount of time.

Loops are helpful because they are going to speed up how long it is going to take you to write out some codes, can help to clean it all up, and can take hundreds of lines of code (potentially), and put it in just a few lines if needed. Think about how much time that is going to save when you can get all of that code into a few lines with the help of the loops.

If you are working on your code and you find that there are parts of the program that can repeat them over and over again, at least a few times, then the loops are going to help make this happen. You will be able to get the code to repeat as many times as you would like, without having to rewrite the same codes over and over again.

Let's say that you would like to work on some kind of program that has a multiplication table that is going to go from 1 to 10 and all of the answers that are needed for it. Maybe you would choose to do some of the beginner codes and write it all line by line while wasting a ton of time and making it so that the code looks kind of messy in the process. But you are able to use the idea of a lop and write it out with the help of a few lines. We will explore some of the different options that are available for the loops and using them, while also seeing how you would be able to do the example above in just a few lines.

While this may seem like a complex thing to work within the coding, it is actually pretty easy to work with, and even a beginner is going to be able to write out some of these codes. The way that these codes will work is that it tells the compiler to keep reading the same part of the code until there is some condition that is met. Once that condition is met, the compiler will get out of the loop and start working on the next part of the code.

So, let's say that you are working on a program, and a part of it needs to be able to count from one to ten. You would be able to use the idea of the loop in order to tell the compiler to keep going through the code until it reaches higher than ten. We can take a look at a few of the different examples that you are able to do with the ideas of the loop.

One thing to remember here is that when you write out some of these loops, it is important to set up the conditions in the right manner. It is easy to forget to set up these conditions when you first get started, but if you forget them right from the beginning of the code, then you will end up in a loop that is not going to stop. You will get stuck in a continuous loop because the code doesn't know when it needs to stop going through the loop.

When you decide to work with some of the methods that are considered more traditional with coding, or using some of the other methods that are found throughout this guidebook, your whole goal here will be to write out all of the lines of code to get things done. Even if you see some parts of the code repeating, then you would still need to rewrite it out. This could take a long time and may not be as easy to work with as well. But when you work with loops, this is not going to be something that is going to be that big of a deal.

When working with these loops, you are able to get rid of some of the traditional ways of coding and change it up and make things easier. You will be able to combine together a ton of lines of code, or as many as you would need in order to get things done. The compiler will still be able to read through it when the loop is done in the proper way, just as long as you make sure that all of your conditions are put in place.

Now that we have spent some time looking at what the loops mean and why they are going to be so important to your code writing, it is time to divide up some of the different types of loops that are available to help you get this done inside the codes you write.

The first loop: the while loop

So, the first type of loop that we are going to explore is the idea of the while loop in Python. This loop is a good one to bring out and use when you want to make sure that your code is able to go through the loop or the cycle for a predetermined number of times. You can pick out how many times you would like the code to go through this kind of loop to get the best results out of it. This makes it easy to get the number of times you would like the loop to go through.

When you work with the while loop, the goal is not to make the code that you write go through the cycle an indefinite amount of times. But you do have in mind a number of times that you would like the code to do its work. So, if you want to count from one to ten in the code, your goal is to use the while loop in order to go through the loop that many times.

With the while loop, you will see that the code is going to go through the loop, and then it will double check to see if the conditions are met or not. Then, if the conditions are not met, they will go through the loop again and then check again. It will continue doing this over and over again until it has met the conditions, and then it will go on to the other part of the code when the loop is all gone.

To see how the while loop is going to work, and to gain a better understanding of the loop works in general, let's look at some examples of a code that has a while loop inside of it:

counter = 1

while(counter <= 3):

principal = int(input("Enter the principal amount:"))

numberofyeras = int(input("Enter the number of years:"))

rateofinterest = float(input("Enter the rate of interest:"))

simpleinterest = principal * numberofyears * rateofinterest/100

```
print("Simple interest = %.2f" %simpleinterest)

#increase the counter by 1

counter = counter + 1

print("You have calculated simple interest for 3 times!")
```

Before we take a look at some of the other types of loops that we are able to work with, let's open up the compiler on Python and type in the code to see what is going to happen when we execute it. You will then be able to see how the while loop is able to work. The program is able to go through and figure out the interest rates, along with the final amounts that are associated with it, based on the numbers that the user, or you, will put into the system.

With the example from the code that was above, we have the loop set up so that it is going to go through three times. This means that the user gets a chance to put in different numbers and see the results three times, and then the system will be able to move on. You do get the chance to add in more or take out some loops based on what is the best for your needs.

The second loop: the for loop

At this point, we have been able to take a look at the while loop and what it is all going to entail, it is time to take a look at the for loop so that we are able to see how this in order to do more with loops, and how this is going to be different than the while loop overall. When you work with the while loops, you will notice that the code is going to go through a loop a certain number of times. But it is not always going to work for all of the situations where you want to bring in a loop. And the for loop is going to help us to fill in the blanks that the while loop is not able to do.

When you are ready to work with the for loop, you will be able to set up the code in a manner that the user isn't going to be the one who will go into the code and provide the program with the information that it needs. They do not have the control that is needed to stop the loop from running.

Instead of the user being able to hold the control, the for loop is going to be set up so that it will go over the iteration of your choice in the order that you place the items into your code. This information, when the for loop is going to list them out in the exact way that they are listed in the code. The user will not need to input anything for the for loop to work.

A good example of how this is going to work inside your code so that you are able to make it work for your needs will include the following syntax:

```
# Measure some strings:
words = ['apple,' 'mango,' 'banana,' 'orange']
for w in words:
print(w, len(w))
```

When you work with the for loop example that is above, you are able to add it to your compiler and see what happens when it gets executed. When you do this, the four fruits that come out on your screen will show up in the exact order that you have them written out. If you would like to have them show up in a different order, you can do that, but then you need to go back to your code and rewrite them in the right order, or your chosen order. Once you have then written out in the syntax and they are ready to be executed in the code, you can't make any changes to them.

The third loop: the nested loop

The third and final loop that we are going to work within Python is going to be known as the nested loop. You will find that when we look at the nested loop, there are going to be some parts that are similar to what we looked at with the while loop and with the for loop, but it is going to use these topics in a different way. when you decide to work with a nested loop, you will just take one loop, and then make sure that it is placed inside of another loop. Then, both of these loops will work together and continue on with their work until both have had a chance to finish.

This may seem really hard to work with when it comes to the loops, and you may wonder if there is actually any time that you, as a beginner, would need to work with this loop. But there are often a lot more chances to work with the nested loop than you may think in the beginning. For example, if you are working some kind of code that needs to have a multiplication table inside of it, and you want the answers listed all the way up, then you are going to work with the nested loop.

Imagine how long this kind of process is going to take if you have to go out and list each and every part of the code without using a loop to make it happen. You would have to write out the lines of codes to do one time one, one's times two, and so on until you reach the point where you are at ten times ten. This would end up being a ton of lines of code just to make this kind of table work in your code. But you are able to work with the idea of the nested loop in order to see the results that you want.

A good example that you will be able to work with to show how a nested loop works and to make sure that you are able to make a full multiplication table of your own, includes the following:

#write a multiplication table from 1 to 10

For x in xrange(1, 11):

```
For y in xrange(1, 11):

Print '%d = %d' % (x, y, x*x)
```

When you got the output of this program, it is going to look similar to this:

```
1*1 = 1

1*2 = 2

1*3 = 3

1*4 = 4
```

All the way up to 1*10 = 2

Then it would move on to do the table by twos such as this:

```
2*1 =2

2*2 = 4
```

And so on until you end up with 10*10 = 100 as your final spot in the sequence.

Go ahead and put this into the compiler and see what happens. You will simply have four lines of code, and end up with a whole multiplication table that shows up on your program. Think of how many lines of code you would have to write out to get this table the traditional way that you did before? This table only took a few lines to accomplish, which shows how powerful and great the nested loop can be.

As you can see, there are a lot of different things that you are able to do when you start to implement some loops into the codes that you are writing. There are a ton of reasons why you should add a loop into the code you are writing. You will be able to use it in most cases to take a large amount of code and write it in just a few lines instead. This saves you time, cleans up the code that you are trying to light, and the compiler is going to be able to still help you do some things that are super powerful!

Chapter 6: K-Means Clustering

Clustering falls under the category of unsupervised machine learning algorithms. It is often applied when the data is not labeled. The goal of the algorithm is to identify clusters or groups within the data.

The idea behind the clusters is that the objects contained one cluster is more related to one another than the objects in the other clusters. The similarity is a metric reflecting the strength of the relationship between two data objects. Clustering is highly applied in exploratory data mining. In have many uses in diverse fields such as pattern recognition, machine learning, information retrieval, image analysis, data compression, bio-informatics, and computer graphics.

The algorithm forms clusters of data based on the similarity between data values. You are required to specify the value of K, which are the number of clusters that you expect the algorithm to make from the data. The algorithm first selects a centroid value for every cluster. After that, it performs three steps in an iterative manner:

1. Calculate the Euclidian distance between every data instance and the centroids for all clusters.
2. Assign the instances of data to the cluster of centroid with the nearest distance.
3. **Calculate the new centroid values depending on the mean values of the coordinates of the data instances from the corresponding cluster.**

Let us manually demonstrate how this algorithm works before implementing it on Scikit-Learn:

Suppose we have two dimensional data instances given below and by the name D:

D = { (5,3), (10,15), (15,12), (24,10), (30,45), (85,70), (71,80), (60,78), (55,52), (80,91) }

Our goal is to divide the data into two clusters, namely C1 and C2 depending on the similarity between the data points.

We should first initialize the values for the centroids of both clusters, and this should be done randomly. The centroids will be named C1 and C2 for clusters C1 and C2 respectively, and we will initialize them with the values for the first two data points, that is, (5,3) and (10,15). It is after this that you should begin the iterations.

Anytime that you calculate the Euclidean distance, the data point should be assigned to the cluster with the shortest Euclidean distance. Let us take the example of the data point (5,3):

Euclidean Distance from the Cluster Centroid C1 = (5,3) = 0

Euclidean Distance from the Cluster Centroid C2 = (10,15) = 13

The Euclidean distance for the data point from point centroid c1 is shorter compared to the distance of the same data point from centroid C2. This means that this data point will be assigned to the cluster C1.

Let us take another data point, (15,12):

Euclidean Distance from the Cluster Centroid C1 = (5,3) IS 13.45

Euclidean Distance from the Cluster Centroid C2 = (10,15) IS 5.83

The distance from the data point to the centroid C2 is shorter, hence it will be assigned to the cluster C2.

Now that the data points have been assigned to the right clusters, the next step should involve calculation of the new centroid values. The values should be calculated by determining the means of the coordinates for the data points belonging to a certain cluster.

If for example for C1 we had allocated the following two data points to the cluster:

(5, 3) and (24, 10). The new value for x coordinate will be the mean of the two:

x = (5 + 24) / 2

x = 14.5

The new value for y will be:

y = (3 + 10) / 2

y = 13/2

y = 6.5

The new centroid value for the c1 will be (14.5, 6.5).

This should be done for c2 and the entire process be repeated. The iterations should be repeated until when the centroid values do not update any more. This means if for example, you do three iterations, you may find that the updated values for centroids c1 and c2 in the fourth iterations are equal to what we had in iteration 3. This means that your data cannot be clustered any further.

You are now familiar with how the K-Means algorithm works. Let us discuss how you can implement it in the Scikit-Learn library.

Let us first import all the libraries that we need to use:

import matplotlib.pyplot as plt

import numpy as np

from sklearn.cluster import KMeans

Data Preparation

We should now prepare the data that is to be used. We will be creating a **numpy array** with a total of 10 rows and 2 columns. So, why have we chosen to work with a numpy array? It is because Scikit-Learn library can work with the numpy array data inputs without the need for preprocessing. Let us create it:

X = np.array([[5,3], [10,15], [15,12], [24,10], [30,45], [85,70], [71,80], [60,78], [55,52], [80,91],])

Visualizing the Data

Now that we have the data, we can create a plot and see how the data points are distributed. We will then be able to tell whether there are any clusters at the moment:

plt.scatter(X[:,0],X[:,1], label='True Position')

    plt.show()

The code gives the following plot:

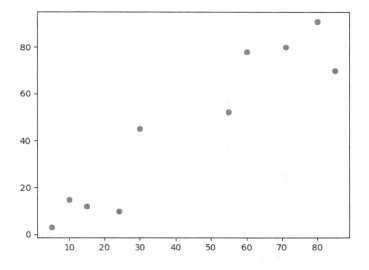

If we use our eyes, we will probably make two clusters from the above data, one at the bottom with five points and another one at the top with five points. We now need to investigate whether this is what the K-Means clustering algorithm will do.

Creating Clusters

We have seen that we can form two clusters from the data points, hence the value of K is now 2. These two clusters can be created by running the following code:

```
kmeans_clusters = KMeans(n_clusters=2)

kmeans_clusters.fit(X)
```

We have created an object named *kmeans_clusters* and 2 have been used as the value for the parameter *n_clusters*. We have then called the *fit()* method on this object and passed the data we have in our numpy array as the parameter to the method.

We can now have a look at the centroid values that the algorithm has created for the final clusters:

```
print (kmeans_clusters.cluster_centers_)
```

This returns the following:

```
[[ 16.8   17. ]
 [ 70.2   74.2]]
```

The first row above gives us the coordinates for the first centroid, which is, (16.8, 17). The second row gives us the coordinates of the second centroid, which is, <u>(70.2,</u> <u>74.2).</u> If you followed the manual process of calculating the values of these, they should be the same. This will be an indication that the K-Means algorithm worked well.

The following script will help us see the data point labels:

print(kmeans_clusters.labels_)

This returns the following:

```
[0 0 0 0 0 1 1 1 1 1]
```

The above output shows a one-dimensional array of 10 elements which correspond to the clusters that are assigned to the 10 data points. You clearly see that we first have a sequence of zeroes which shows that the first 5 points have been clusterd together while the last five points have been clustered together. Note that the 0 and 1 have no mathematical significance but they have simply been used to represent the cluster IDs. If we had three clusters, then the last one would have been represented using 2's.

We can now plot the data points and see how they have been clustered. We need to plot the data points alongside their assigned labels to be able to distinguish the clusters. Just execute the script given below:

```
plt.scatter(X[:,0],X[:,1],    c=kmeans_clusters.labels_,
cmap='rainbow')

    plt.show()
```

The script returns the following plot:

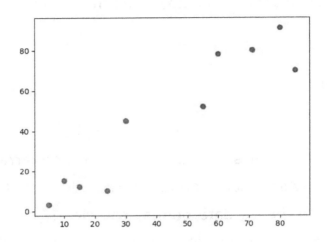

We have simply plotted the first column of the array named X against the second column. At the same time, we have passed *kmeans_labels_* as the value for parameter c which corresponds to the labels. Note the use of the parameter *cmap='rainbow'*. This parameter helps us to choose the color type for the different data points.

As you expected, the first five points have been clustered together at the bottom left and assigned a similar color. The remaining five points have been clustered together at the top right and assigned one unique color.

We can choose to plot the points together with the centroid coordinates for every cluster to see how the positioning of the centroid affects clustering. Let us use three clusters to see how they affect the centroids. The following script will help you to create the plot:

plt.scatter(X[:,0], X[:,1], c=kmeans_clusters.labels_, cmap='rainbow')

plt.scatter(kmeans_clusters.cluster_centers_[:,0] ,kmeans_clusters.cluster_centers_[:,1], color='black')

   plt.show()

The script returns the following plot:

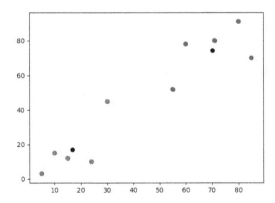

We have chosen to plot the centroid points in black color.

Chapter 7: Support Vector Machines

SVMs fall under the category of supervised machine learning algorithms and are highly applied classification and regression problems. It is known for its ability to handle nonlinear input spaces. It is highly applied in applications like intrusion detection, face detection, classification of news articles, emails and web pages, handwriting recognition and classification of genes.

The algorithm works by segregating the data points in the best way possible. The distance between the nearest points is referred to as the *margin*. The goal is to choose a hyperplane with the maximum possible margin between the support vectors in a given dataset.

To best understand how this algorithm works, let us first implement it in Scikit-Learn library. Our goal is to predict whether a bank currency note is fake or authentic. We will use the attributes of the note including variance of the image, the skewness of the wavelet transformed image, curtosis of the image and entropy of the image.

Since this is a binary classification algorithm, let us use the SVM classification algorithm.

If we have a linearly separable data with two dimensions, the goal of a typical machine learning algorithm is to identify a boundary that will divide the data so as to minimize the misclassification error. In most cases, one gets several lines with all these lines correctly classifying the data.

SVM is different from the other classification algorithms in the way it selects the decision boundary maximizing the distance from the nearest data points for all classes. The goal of SVM is not to find the decision boundary only, but to find the most optimal decision boundary.

The most optimal decision boundary refers to the decision boundary with the maximum margin from nearest points of all classes. The nearest points from the decision boundary maximizing the distance between the decision boundary and the points are known as *support vectors*. For the case of support vector machines, the decision boundary is known as *maximum margin classifier* **or** *maximum margin hyper plane.*

A complex mathematics is involved in the calculation of the support vectors; determine the margin between the decision boundary and support vectors and maximizing the margin.

Let us begin by importing the necessary libraries:

import numpy as np

import pandas as pd

import matplotlib.pyplot as plt

This dataset can be downloaded from the following URL:

https://drive.google.com/file/d/13nw-uRXPY8XIZQxKRNZ3yYlho-CYm_Qt/view

Download and store it on your local machine. I have saved the file in the same directory as my Python scripts and given it the name *bank_note.csv*.

Importing the Dataset

We will use the *read_csv* method provided by the Pandas library to read the data and import it into our workspace. This can be done as follows:

dataset = pd.read_csv("bank_note.csv")

Let us call the **shape** method to print the shape of the data for us:

```
print(dataset.shape)
```

This returns the following:

```
(1372, 5)
```

This shows that there are 1372 columns and 5 columns in the dataset. Let us print the first 5 rows of the dataset:

```
print(dataset.head())
```

Again, this may return an error because of lack of the output information. Let us solve this using the Python's sys library. You should now have the following code:

import numpy as np

import pandas as pd

import matplotlib.pyplot as plt

import sys

```
sys.__stdout__=sys.stdout
```
dataset = pd.read_csv("bank_note.csv")

```
print(dataset.head())
```

The code returns the following output:

	Variance	Skewness	Curtosis	Entropy	Class
0	3.62160	8.6661	-2.8073	-0.44699	0
1	4.54590	8.1674	-2.4586	-1.46210	0
2	3.86600	-2.6383	1.9242	0.10645	0
3	3.45660	9.5228	-4.0112	-3.59440	0
4	0.32924	-4.4552	4.5718	-0.98880	0

All attributes of the data are numeric as shown above. Even the last attribute is numeric as its values are either 0 or 1.

Preprocessing the Data

It is now time to subdivide the above data into attributes and labels as well as training and test sets. The following code will help us subdivide the data into attributes and labels:

X = dataset.drop('Class', axis=1)

y = dataset['Class']

The first line above helps us store all the columns of the dataset into variable **X**, except the *class* column. The *drop()* function has helped us exclude the *Class* column from this. The second line has then helped us store the *Class* column into variable *y*. The variable **X** now has attributes while the variable *y* now has the corresponding labels.

We have achieved the goal of diving the dataset into attributes and labels. The next step is to divide the dataset into training and test sets. Scikit-learn has a library known as *model_selection* which provides us with a method named *train_test_split* that we can use to divide the data into training and test sets.

First, let us import the *train_test_split* method:

from sklearn.model_selection import train_test_split

The following script will then help us to perform the split:

X_train, X_test, y_train, y_test = train_test_split(X, y, test_size = 0.20)

Training the Algorithm

Now that the data has been split into training and test sets, we should now train the SVM on the training set. Scikit-Learn comes with a library known as *svm* which has built-in classes for various SVM algorithms.

In this case, we will be doing a classification task, hence we will use the support vector classifier class (SVC). The takes a single parameter, that is, the kernel type. For a simple SVM, the parameter should be set to **"linear"** since the simple SVMs can only classify data that is linearly separable.

We will call the *fit* method of SVC to train the algorithm on our training set. The training set should be passed as a parameter to the *fit* method. Let us first import the SVC class from Scikit-Learn:

from sklearn.svm import SVC

Now run the following code:

svc_classifier = SVC(kernel='linear')

svc_classifier.fit(X_train, y_train)

Making Predicting

We should use the SVC class for making predictions. Note that the predictions will be made on the test data. Here is the code for making predictions:

pred_y = svc_classifier.predict(X_test)

Evaluating the Accuracy of the Algorithm

In classification tasks, we use confusion matrix, recall, precision and F1 as the metrics. Scikit-Learn has the *metrics* library which provides us with the *confusion_matrix* and *classification_report* methods which can help us find the values of these metrics. The following code can help us find the value for these metrics:

First, let us import the above methods from the Scikit-Learn library:

from sklearn.metrics import confusion_matrix, classification_report

Here is the code that can help in doing the evaluation:

print(confusion_matrix(y_test,pred_y))

print(classification_report(y_test,pred_y))

The code returns the following:

```
[[160    1]
 [   1 113]]
              precision    recall  f1-score   support

           0       0.99      0.99      0.99       161
           1       0.99      0.99      0.99       114

avg / total       0.99      0.99      0.99       275
```

The output given above shows that the algorithm did a good task. An average of 99% for the above metrics is not bad.

Let us give another example of how to implement SVM in Scikit-Learn using the Iris dataset. We had already loaded the Iris dataset, a dataset that shows details of flowers in terms of sepal and petal measurements, that is, width and length. We can now learn from the data, and then make a prediction for unknown data. These calls for us to create an estimator then call its fit method.

This is demonstrated in the script given below:

```
from sklearn import svm

from sklearn import datasets

# Loading the dataset

iris = datasets.load_iris()

clf = svm.LinearSVC()

# learn from the dataset

clf.fit(iris.data, iris.target)

# predict unseen data

clf.predict([[ 6.2,  4.2,  3.5,  0.35]])

# Changing model parameters using the attributes
ending with an underscore

print(clf.coef_ )
```

The code will return the following output:

```
[[ 0.18423824   0.45123312  -0.80793878  -0.45071592]
 [ 0.05187834  -0.88969839   0.40345845  -0.93664852]
 [-0.85062306  -0.98667154   1.38105171   1.86536558]]
```

We now have the predicted values for our data. Note that we imported both *datasets* and *svm* from the scikit-learn library. After loading the dataset, a model was fitted/created by learning patterns from the data. This was done by calling the *fit()* method. Note that the *LinearSVC()* method helps us to create an estimator for the support vector classifier, on which we are to create the model. We have then passed in new data for which we need to make a prediction.

Chapter 8: Variables and Data Types

A software application consists of two fundamental parts: Logic and Data. Logic consists of the functionalities that are applied on data to accomplish a particular task. Application data can be stored in memory or hard disk. Files and databases are used to store data on hard disk. In memory, data is stored in the form of variables.

Definition of Variable

Variable in programming is a memory location used to store some value. Whenever you store a value in a variable, that value is actually being stored at physical location in memory. Variables can be thought of as reference to physical memory location. The size of the memory reserved for a variable depends upon the type of value stored in the variable.

Creating a Variable

It is very easy to create a variable in Python. The assignment operator "=" is used for this purpose. The value to the left of the assignment operator is the variable identifier or name of the variable. The value to the right of the operator is the value assigned to the variable. Take a look at the following code snippet.

```
Name  = 'Mike'       # A string variable

Age   = 15          # An integer variable

Score = 102.5       # A floating type variable

Pass  = True        # A boolean Variable
```

In the script above we created four different types of variables. You can see that we did not specify the type of variable with the variable name. For instance we did not write "string Name" or "int Age". We only wrote the variable name. This is because Python is a loosely typed language. Depending upon the value being stored in a variable, Python assigns type to the variable at runtime. For instance when Python interpreter interprets the line "Age = 15", it checks the type of the value which is integer in this case. Hence, Python understands that Age is an integer type variable.

To check type of a variable, pass the variable name to "type" function as shown below:

```
type(Age)
```

You will see that the above script, when run, prints "int" in the output which is basically the type of Age variable.

Python allows multiple assignment which means that you can assign one value to multiple variables at the same time. Take a look at the following script:

Age = Number = Point = 20 #Multiple Assignment

print (Age)

print (Number)

print (Point)

In the script above, integer 20 is assigned to three variables: Age, Number and Point. If you print the value of these three variables, you will see 20 thrice in the output.

Python Data Types

A programming application needs to store variety of data. Consider scenario of a banking application that needs to store customer information. For instance, a person's name and mobile number; whether he is a defaulter or not; collection of items that he/she has loaned and so on. To store such variety of information, different data types are required. While you can create custom data types in the form of classes, Python provides six standard data types out of the box. They are:

- Strings
- Numbers
- Booleans
- Lists
- Tuples
- Dictionaries

Strings

Python treats string as sequence of characters. To create strings in Python, you can use single as well as double quotes. Take a look at the following script:

first_name = 'mike' # String with single quotation

last_name = " johns" # String with double quotation

full_name = first_name + last_name # string concatenation using +

print(full_name)

In the above script we created three string variables: first_name, last_name and full_name. String with single quotes is used to initialize the variable "first_name" while string with double quotes initializes the variable "last_name". The variable full_name contains the concatenation of the first_name and last_name variables. Running the above script returns following output:

mike johns

Numbers

There are four types of numeric data in python:

- int (Stores integer e.g 10)
- float (Stores floating point numbers e.g 2.5)
- long (Stores long integer such as 48646684333)
- complex (Complex number such as 7j+4847k)

To create a numeric Python variable, simply assign a number to variable. In the following script we create four different types of numeric objects and print them on the console.

```
int_num = 10      # integer

float_num = 156.2  #float

long_num = -0.5977485613454646  #long

complex_num = -.785+7J #Complex
```

```
print(int_num)
```

```
print(float_num)
```

```
print(long_num)
```

```
print(complex_num)
```

The output of the above script will be as follows:

```
10
156.2
-0.5977485613454646
(-0.785+7j)
```

Boolean

Boolean variables are used to store Boolean values. True and False are the two Boolean values in Python. Take a look at the following example:

```
defaulter = True
```

```
has_car = False
```

```
print(defaulter and has_car)
```

In the script above we created two Boolean variables "defaulter" and "has_car" with values True and False respectively. We then print the result of the AND operation on both of these variables. Since the AND operation between True and False returns false, you will see false in the output. We will study more about the logical operators in the next chapter.

Lists

In Python, List data type is used to store collection of values. Lists are similar to arrays in any other programming language. However Python lists can store values of different types. To create a list opening and closing square brackets are used. Each item in the list is separated from the other with a comma. Take a look at the following example.

```
cars = ['Honda', 'Toyota', 'Audi', 'Ford', 'Suzuki', 'Mercedez']

print(len(cars))   #finds total items in string

print(cars)
```

In the script above we created a list named cars. The list contains six string values i.e. car names. Next we printed the size of the list using len function. Finally we print the list on console.

The output looks like this:

```
6
['Honda', 'Toyota', 'Audi', 'Ford', 'Suzuki', 'Mercedez']
```

Tuples

Tuples are similar to lists with two major differences. Firstly, opening and closing braces are used to create tuples instead of lists that use square brackets. Secondly, tuple once created is immutable which means that you cannot change tuple values once it is created. The following example clarifies this concept.

cars = ['Honda', 'Toyota', 'Audi', 'Ford', 'Suzuki', 'Mercedez']

cars2 = ('Honda', 'Toyota', 'Audi', 'Ford', 'Suzuki', 'Mercedez')

cars [3] = 'WV'

cars2 [3] = 'WV'

In the above script we created a list named cars and a tuple named cars2. Both the list and tuple contains list of car names. We then try to update the third index of the list as well as tuple with a new value. The list will be updated but an error will be thrown while trying to update the tuple's third index. This is due to the fact that tuple, once created cannot be modified with new values. The error looks like this:

```
TypeError                                 Traceback (most recent call last)
<ipython-input-17-d971617cbfe4> in <module>()
      5 cars [3] = 'WW'
----> 7 cars2 [3] = 'WW'

TypeError: 'tuple' object does not support item assignment
```

Dictionaries

Dictionaries store collection of data in the form of key-value pairs. Each key-value pair is separated from the other via comma. Keys and values are separated from each other via colon. Dictionary items can be accessed via index as well as keys. To create dictionaries you need to add key-value pairs inside opening and closing parenthesis. Take a look at the following example.

cars = {'Name':'Audi', 'Model': 2008, 'Color':'Black'}

print(cars['Color'])

print(cars.keys())

print(cars.values())

In the above script we created a dictionary named cars. The dictionary contains three key-value pairs i.e. 3 items. To access value, we can pass key to the brackets that follow dictionary name. Similarly we can use keys() and values() methods to retrieve all the keys and values from a dictionary, respectively. The output of the script above looks like this:

```
Black
dict_keys(['Name', 'Model', 'Color'])
dict_values(['Audi', 2008, 'Black'])
```

Chapter 9: How to install the Python Interpreter, how to use the Python Shell, IDLE and write your first program ✐

Python installation is dependent upon the OS on your computer as well as the source of the Python installation you are using. Python can be obtained from a number of different sources, some of which are modified versions of the official releases.

The following discussion will look at the installation procedure for the 3 major supported operating systems from the official source at python.org. Installation for other operating systems should be similar to one of these three. Please see python.org for installers and instructions for those systems.

The installers on pythons.org contain the python interpreter, the IDLE integrated development environment and the python shell.

Following is an OS specific description to installing and accessing each.

Mac OS X:

Mac OS X comes with Python 2 preinstalled. The exact version of python will depend on the version of OS X currently running on your system and can be determined by opening the terminal app and entering the following at the prompt:

python –V

which should return a result similar to:

Python 2.6.1

Python 3 can also be installed on OS X with no need to uninstall 2.x. To check for a 3.x installation open the terminal app and enter the following at the prompt:

Python3 –V

which should return a result similar to:

Python 3.6.4

By default, OS X will not have python 3.x installed. If you wish to use python 3.x, it can be installed with binary installers for OS X available at python.org.

Those installers will install the interpreter, the IDLE development tools and the python shell for python 3.x. Unlike python 2.x, those tools are installed as standard applications in the applications folder.

Running IDLE and the python shell in OS X is dependent on the version of Python you are using and your personal preference. The IDLE/shell applications in Python 2.x and 3.x can be started from the terminal window by entering the following commands:

For python 2.x:

Idle

For Python 3.x:

idle3

As mentioned above, Python 3 also installs IDLE as a standard application in the Python folder within the Applications older. To start the IDLE/Shell program from the desktop simply open that folder and double click the IDLE application.

Python can also be accessed as a command line terminal application within OS X. With a terminal window open, simply enter the following:

Python 2.x:

Python

and you will get a response like:

Python 2.6.1 (r261:67515, Jun 24 2010, 21:47:49)
[GCC 4.2.1 (Apple Inc. build 5646)] on darwin
Type "help", "copyright", "credits" or "license" for more information.

>>>

Python 3.x:

python3

and you will get a response like:

Python 3.6.4 (v3.6.4:d48ecebad5, Dec 18 2017, 21:07:28)
[GCC 4.2.1 (Apple Inc. build 5666) (dot 3)] on darwin
Type "help", "copyright", "credits" or "license" for more information.

>>>

The >>> prompt allows direct entry of python commands which will be detailed in greater depth later.

Windows:

Once setup correctly, python can used from the command line with either command.exe or the windows power shell.

Alternatively, the standard installation adds Python IDLE to the start menu. Selecting that will bring up the IDLE application to allow you to start creating your first script.

Linux

If you are using one of the many flavors of Linux you can check for the presence of python by typing

python -V

at a shell command prompt. If python is installed, the installed version should be returned like

Python 3.6.4

If not, an error should be returned.

Installing and/or updating can vary depending on the Linux distribution you are using. Please consult the documentation for your linux distribution for more information.

Python Interpreter, IDLE, and the Shell

A standard installation of Python from python.org, contains documentation, licensing information and 3 main executable files which are used to develop and run python scripts.

Let's take a brief look at each of these three programs and the role each plays in python programming.

Python Interpreter

The python interpreter is the program responsible for executing the scripts you write. The interpreter converts the .py script files into bytecode instructions and then processes them according to the code written in the file.

Python IDLE

IDLE is the Python integrated development and learning environment. It contains all of the tools you will need to develop programs in Python including the shell, a text editor and debugging tools.

Depending on your python version and operating system, IDLE can be very basic or have an extensive array of options that can be setup.

For example, on Mac OS X, the text editor can be setup with several code indentation and highlighting options which can make your programs much easier to read and work with.

If the text editor in IDLE does not offer the sophistication you need, there are several aftermarket text editors which support Python script highlighting, autocomplete and other features that make script writing easier.

<u>Python Shell</u>

The shell is an interactive, command line driven interface to the python interpreter.

In the python shell, commands are entered at the >>> prompt. Anything that is entered at the prompt must be in proper python syntax, incorrect entries will return a syntax error like

SyntaxError: invalid syntax

When a command is entered, it is specific to that shell and has the lifetime of the shell.

For example, if you assign a variable a value such as:

>>>X=10

Then the variable is assigned an integer value of 10.

That value will be maintained until the shell is closed, restarted or the value is changed.

If another shell window is opened, the value of X will not be accessible in the new window.

When a command is entered and accepted, the code is executed. If the entered code generates a response, the response will be output to the specified device. If it does not, such as simply assigning a variable as above, then another prompt (>>>) is shown and additional commands can be entered.

This can be useful for a number of simple tasks, testing simple functions and getting a feel for how commands work.

As an example, enter the following:

```
>>>X=10
>>>Y=5
>>>print(X)
10
>>>print(Y)
5
>>>print(X+Y)
15
```

This demonstrates a couple of things.
First, we assign the two variables X and Y values.

Both variables retain their values within the shell. It also shows that the way we defined the variables was acceptable. If it is acceptable in the shell, it will be acceptable in a script.

If a command is not acceptable, it will return an error or exception.

For example if we ask for the length of X with the following command

```
>>>print(len(X))
```

Then the following is returned:

```
Traceback (most recent call last):
  File "<pyshell#12>", line 1, in <module>
    print(len(X))
 TypeError: object of type 'int' has no len()
```

The error returned usually will provide some valuable information as to why the error occurred.

In this case, it is telling us that we assigned an integer value to X.

The len() command gives the length of a string so we are getting this error because the type of data held by the variable does not match the requirements of the function called.

If instead we had used

```
>>>print(len(str(X)))
 2
```

In this case, we are using the str() command to convert the value of X into a string.

We are then using len() to get the length of that string, which is 2 characters.

This can be loosely translated into

$$X=12 \Rightarrow str(X)='12' \Rightarrow len('12')=2$$

We can continue to use the shell to explore other things like different ways to assign variable values.

For example, rather than explicitly assigning values on a per line basis, variables can be assigned as comma separated groups.

```
>>>X,Y = 20,12
 >>>print(X,Y)
 20 12
```

Script Editor

To create our first program, open the text editor.

To open it in a GUI OS like OS X or Windows, select File->New from the IDLE menus.

In non-GUI implementations .py files can be created in a terminal text editor like VI or VIM. Please see documentation on those programs for information on working in them.

Once a text window is open we can simply enter our program code.

In this case, we will write a quick program for calculating the volume of a cylinder. The formula is V=(πr^2)*h where r is the radius and h is the height.

While this program will be extremely simple, and could easily be done just using the shell, it will show several fundamentally important things in Python programming.

The first step will be to import the math library.

Many functions available in python are stored in libraries. These libraries typically house functions which are grouped by task such as math.

If the proper library is not loaded when prior to making a call to that library, an error such as

Traceback (most recent call last):
   File "<pyshell#22>", line 1, in <module>
     print(math.exp(2))
  NameError: name 'math' is not defined

will be displayed. This error is telling you that math is not defined.

Since math is part of a Python standard library this tells you that the library was not imported prior to execution of the request for the math keyword.

In the text editor, enter the lines as follows

```
# import math library
import math
```

The #is the python comment symbol. Anything between that and the end of the line is ignored by the interpreter.

One of the key advantages of Python scripting is readability so it is very important (as it is in all programing) to be diligent about commenting.

Comments will make it easier to debug your code later and will make it easier for someone else to look at your work and see how the program works.

In many cases, it also forces you to slow down and think out the programming process as you go which will lead to cleaner and better organized code.

Next, we need to set up our variables.

This can be done anywhere within a script as long as they are defined prior to calling for their value.

If a variable is called before it is defined, a 'name not defined' exception will be displayed and program execution will halt.

```
# assign variables
```

```
r=5 # radius
h=10 # height
V=0 # volume
```

While V does not need to be explicitly defined, here it is considered good practice to do so because it makes the code is easier to understand.

Next, we do the actual volume calculation.

```
# calculate volume of a cylinder
V=(math.pi*math.pow(r,2))*h # volume=(π*r^2)*h
```

Next, to see the result we use the print function, which will output the result to the console.

```
# output the result
print(V)
```

The complete program looks like this

```
# import math

import math

# assign variables
r=5 # radius
h=10 # height
V=0 # volume
```

```
# calculate volume of a cylinder
V=(math.pi*math.pow(r,2))*h # volume=(π*r^2)*h

# output the result
print(V)
```

You can save the program to your hard drive, let's call it cylinder.py.

Python views files ending in .py as script files so it is important to always save your scripts with the .py extension. Once we have a saved script file, we can go ahead and run it.

Chapter 10: Strings

Earlier in the variables section we learned a little about strings. Strings and string functions are one of the strengths of the Python language.

It has many built in string handling and manipulation features and many more are available through external libraries. Previously, we discussed accessing substrings using the [:] nomenclature, as well as concatenating strings using the '+' operator.

Python offers inline string formatting similar to that in C/C++ through the use of the % special character. % followed by any one of a number of formatting characters allows variable information to be inserted into formatted strings for display or storage.

Those special characters include:

%c – character
%d – signed decimal
%e – lower case e exponent
%E – upper case E exponent
%f – floating point number
%g – the smaller of %e/%f
%G – the smaller of %E/%F

%i – signed integer

%s – string

%u – unsigned integer

%o – octal

%x – lower case hexadecimal

%X – upper case hexadecimal

These can be used as follows to format text on the fly:

>>> print('%s scored %i in game one of the playoffs' % ('John', 32))

John scored 32 in game one of the playoffs

As shown the values for %s and %i are dynamically inserted into the output text based on the input values provided in parenthesis.

While in this example, the values are given explicitly, they can also be provided as variables. Care must be taken to insure the variable types and the formatting characters match. In other words, do not specify %i and provide a string variable as the source.

These formatting characters also have a number of modifiers that alter or specify their output.

These include:

*   specifies width or precision

\-   justify left

+   show sign

<sp>   left padding with spaces

show leading 0's in octal output or leading 0x in hexidecimal

0   left padding with 0's

%%   literal % (allows printing a % symbol in the string)

(var)   key value for dictionary elements

m.n.   for floating point numbers this is the minimum width and number of decimal places

```
>>> print('%s spent $%3.2f at the store last night' % ('John', 12.8975))
```

John spent $12.90 at the store last night

%3.2f formats the floating point number to 2 decimal places.

The % nomenclature is considered the 'old way' of handling string formatting. The new format is to enclose the formatted text in braces while calling the format function like this:

```
>>> print('{} spent ${:2.2f} at the store last night'.format('John', 12.8975))
```

John spent $12.90 at the store last night

In this case, the first insert is a set of empty braces. This is what is classified as an autofill, or more specifically that it is filled by the items in the format command in the order it's called.

The second set of braces then autofills with the second item in the format statement. In that second statement we used a ':' to specify that a formatting modifier is included.

Alternatively, we can manually select which items within the format command get inserted into the string as follows:

>>> print('Item 3={2}, Item 2={1}, Item 4={3}, Item 1={0}'.format('1','2','3','4'))

Item 3=3, Item 2=2, Item 4=4, Item 1=1

A dictionaries key value pair can also be used to fill in strings dynamically as well. For example:

>>> 'My Name is {firstname} and I am {age} years old'.format(firstname='John', age=29)

'My Name is John and I am 29 years old'

Or..

```
>>>    testd={'firstname':    'John',    'age':    29}
>>> 'My Name is {firstname} and I am {age} years
old'.format(**testd)
```

'My Name is John and I am 29 years old'

The ** operator is the exponent operator when applied
to numerical variables. When applied as shown to a
dictionary, it force splits the dictionary into its
component entities.

If testd={'firstname': 'John', 'age': 29} then **testd=(
firstname='John', age=29) so the use of the operator
functionally converts the contents of the dictionary
variable in the second example into the format of the
first example.

Python has a large number of built in string
methods. These do a wide range of everyday string
manipulation functions in a single command that would
require more elaborate programming in other
languages.

As of this writing there are 44 different methods
available and as the language evolves more are
added. Due that evolution, the not all of the 44 will be
available on all versions of Python.

Because of that fact, and the sheer volume of methods, covering all of them and their use is beyond the scope of this book.

Here are a few of the more commonly used examples and how to use them. Reference to all of them is available from the docs on python.org.

str.lower() - converts a string to all lower case

```
>>> str.lower('Hello')
 'hello'
```

str.upper() - converts a string to all upper case

```
>>> str.upper('Hello')
 'HELLO'
```

These functions convert text to all lower or upper case respectively. This is a common operation when checking for non-case sensitive equality in string values.

```
>>> print('Hello'=='hello')
 False
```

```
>>> print(str.lower('Hello')=='hello')
 True
```

str.strip([char]) – strips characters from the beginning and end of a string. It removes only the characters specified by char. If char is not specified, it strips whitespace. This is a commonly used command to remove leading and trailing spaces from user input.

```
>>> print(str.strip('    Hello    '))
 Hello
```

```
>>> print(str.strip('    #--Comments--#    ', ' #-'))
 Comments
```

str.split([,delimiter]) – splits a string into individual list entries using delimiter as the split point.

```
>>> str.split('A,b,CC,ASD,The end', ',')
 ['A', 'b', 'CC', 'ASD', 'The end']
```

```
>>> str.split('www.mywebsite.com', '.')
 ['www', 'mywebsite', 'com']
```

```
>>> myweb='WWW.WEBSITE.COM'
 >>> myweb.split('.')
 ['www', 'website', 'com']
```

Chapter 11: Control Flow
Introduction

Went to sleep you starts execution of the program code, it starts from the main function and terminates at the end of the code, which is usually the end of main function. The statements that are executed in sequence are nothing but the part of the program. Most of the programs, which we have learned until now are simple straight line programs. These programs have a steady and sequential flow.

To break the flow of control, we have control flow statements in C++. Please control flow statements help the programmer to change the path of the CPU. Some of the control flow statements discussed below.

Halt: this is the most widely used and the basic control statement in C++. You can perform a halt with the exit function. The exit functional is defined in the header cstdlib. Here is a small example showing the use of exit function.

```
1  #include <cstdlib> // needed for exit()
2  #include <iostream>
3  int main()
4  {
5      std::cout << 1;
6      exit(0); // terminate and return 0 to operating system
7      // The following statements never execute
8      std::cout << 2;
9      return 0;
10 }
```

In the above sample code the flow of control is broken and it will never reach the statements that are written below the exit statement. These types of statements give the programmer the authority to stop the program when required.

Jumps: Jump is also a basic controls statement in C++. Using this statement will make the CPU to jump to a different statement. Continue, break and goto are used to perform different types of jumping operations.

Conditional branches: these are flow control statements which change the part of the flow of control depending on the value of a given expression. The 'if' statement is the most basic type of the conditional branch statements. Example:

```
1  int main()
2  {
3      // do A
4      if (expression)
5          // do B
6      else
7          // do C
8      // do D
9  }
```

In the sample code given above, there are two possible paths the flow of control can take. If it is it true the CPU will go and execute A, B and D. But if the condition turns out to be false the flow of control will go and execute A, C and D statements.

Conditionals

Conditionals allow you to form a junction in the code and send it off on various paths, rather than keeping it as a linear code. C++ conditionals are if statements - if something is false, the program should execute one piece of code, another if it is true:

```
1  int a = 1;
2  {
3   if(a < 2)
4   {
5     cout << "a is less than 2!\n";
6   }
```

You know what lines 1 and 5 mean but line 3 is a little different – this is an if statement. What it is doing is checking to see if the integer variable is less than 2. If it is, it will run one piece of code, if not, it will carry on as normal. If you compile and run what is written here, you will see printed on your screen "a is less than 2!".

Loops

Loops are used in the programs where the code is to be used repeatedly. They will put the code into a loop till the condition is satisfied. Imagine if you have to write a code, which prints numbers from 1 to 100 in a new line each. Writing the code for such programs will be very difficult and time taking. For such situations we use loops. Loops keep the flow of control in the loop till the condition is satisfied.

So our code now reads user inputs, it can do a variety of different things based on those inputs but now we are going to look at making that code do the same things over and over again but with slightly different parameters. To do this, we need to use a loop, which is a piece of code that is repeated a number of different times until it's achieved what it needed to do and a specific C++ condition has been met. C++ has three different types of loop:

- while
- for
- do

The WHILE loop is the easiest and looks very similar to an if statement:

```
1  int userInput = 0;
2
3  while(userInput != 10)
4  {
5      cin >> userInput;
6  }
```

What the WHILE loop is doing here is saying that while whatever the user input variable is not equal to 10, the ode needs to get some input from the user. In C++, the exclamation mark (!) means not, so ! = means not equal.

In this case, if the user input had already been 10 then the code would not have been executed and the loop will be ignored. In all truthfulness, the WHILE loop is just seen as an extended IF statement that goes back inside of itself after the code is run.

Before we move on, I want to show what an INFINITE loop looks like, a loop that just keeps on going:

```
1  while(1 == 1)
2  {
3  cout << "a";
4  }
```

As you can see, it is saying that if 1 is equal to 1, print an a, and so on.

The next easiest loop is the DO WHILE loop, as it is similar to the while loop.

```
1  ⊟int userInput = 0;
2   ⌐
3   do
4   {
5       cin >> userInput;
6   } while (userInput != 10);
```

While it looks somewhat different to the WHILE loop, it is doing essentially the same job with one important difference – the WHILE loop checks a conditional and looks to see if it is true but the DO WHILE loop runs code and then checks if the conditional is true or not. Because of this, all of the code is guaranteed to run.

The third type of C++ loop is FOR and this one is the most complicated one. Once you understand it though, you will find that it is the most powerful. Here, we are just going to look at simple usage:

```
1  ⊟int i = 0;
2   ⌐
3   for(i = 2; i < 10; ++i)
4   {
5       cout << i << "\n";
6   }
```

What this code is saying is, start off by setting the value of i to 2. Then it goes on to say that, as long as i is less than 10 it should output the value onto the screen and then increment i. You must bear one thing in mind – all of the variables that are used in the first line of a FOR loop have to be the same variable. It is also important to remember that, unlike a WHILE loop, the first statement is an assignment and not a conditional.

This sort of loop is useful if you want to get through a number of pieces of data and I'll talk more about that in the next section. For now, as you can see, the most useful thing it can do is chuck out a sequence of numbers. That is a useful talks and it brings us neatly on to the next section.

If statement:

The 'if' statement is the most basic condition right statement in C++. It will check for a given condition and will change the flow of control depending on the outcome of the condition.

Here is a simple code which has an 'if' statement and it.

```
1   #include <iostream>
2   int main()
3   {
4       std::cout << "Enter a number: ";
5       int x;
6       std::cin >> x;
7       if (x > 10)
8           std::cout << x << "is greater than 10\n";
9       else
10          std::cout << x << "is not greater than 10\n";
11      return 0;
12  }
```

We already know that if statement takes a statement as the condition. We also know that we can use a block in place of a single statement. This means we can use a Block inside an if statement as a condition. The following example shows a Block being used in an if statement as a condition.

```
1   #include <iostream>
2   int main()
3   {
4       std::cout << "Enter a number: ";
5       int x;
6       std::cin >> x;
7       if (x > 10)
8           {
9           // both statements will be executed if x > 10
10          std::cout << "You entered " << x << "\n";
11          std::cout << x << "is greater than 10\n";
12          }
13      else
14          {
15          // both statements will be executed if x <= 10
16          std::cout << "You entered " << x << "\n";
17          std::cout << x << "is not greater than 10\n";
18          }
19      return 0;
20  }
```

You can also place one if statement inside another if statement. An if statement which has another if statement in it is called a nested if.

Here are two examples, which will help you to understand the nested if better.

Example 1:

```
1   #include <iostream>
2   using namespace std;
3
4   int main ()
5   {
6       // local variable declaration:
7       int a = 100;
8       int b = 200;
9
10      // check the boolean condition
11      if( a == 100 )
12      {
13          // if condition is true then check the following
14          if( b == 200 )
15          {
16              // if condition is true then print the following
17              cout << "Value of a is 100 and b is 200" << endl;
18          }
19      }
20      cout << "Exact value of a is : " << a << endl;
21      cout << "Exact value of b is : " << b << endl;
22
23      return 0;
24  }
```

Example 2:

```
1   #include <iostream>
2   int main()
3   {
4       std::cout << "Enter a number: ";
5       int x;
6       std::cin >> x;
7       if (x > 10) // outer if statement
8           // it is bad coding style to nest if statements this way
9           if (x < 20) // inner if statement
10              std::cout << x << "is between 10 and 20\n";
11          // who does this else belong to?
12          else
13              std::cout << x << "is greater than 20\n";
14      return 0;
15  }
```

You can encase an if statement into a block and you can attach an else statement to it. You can see how with the below example.

```
1   #include <iostream>
2   int main()
3   {
4       std::cout << "Enter a number: ";
5       int x;
6       std::cin >> x;
7       if (x > 10)
8       {
9           if (x < 20)
10              std::cout << x << "is between 10 and 20\n";
11      }
12      else // attached to outer if statement
13          std::cout << x << "is less than 10\n";
14      return 0;
15  }
```

If statements with logical operators

You can use if statements with logical operators for checking multiple conditions at the same time. The sample code is given below.

Example:

```
1   #include <iostream>
2   int main()
3   {
4       std::cout << "Enter an integer: ";
5       int x;
6       std::cin >> x;
7       std::cout << "Enter another integer: ";
8       int y;
9       std::cin >> y;
10      if (x > 0 && y > 0) // && is logical and -- checks if both conditions are true
11          std::cout << "both numbers are positive\n";
12      else if (x > 0 || y > 0) // || is logical or -- checks if either condition is true
13          std::cout << "One of the numbers is positive\n";
14      else
15          std::cout << "Neither number is positive\n";
16      return 0;
17  }
```

'if' statements can be used for performing early returns. Early returns are nothing but getting the control back to the caller before the Flood control reaches the end of the function.

```
1   enum ErrorCode
2   {
3       ERROR_SUCCESS = 0,
4       ERROR_NEGATIVE_NUMBER = -1
5   };
6   ErrorCode doSomething(int value)
7   {
8       // if value is a negative number
9       if (value < 0)
10          // early return an error code
11          return ERROR_NEGATIVE_NUMBER;
12      // Do whatever here
13      return ERROR_SUCCESS;
14  }
15  int main()
16  {
17      std::cout << "Enter a positive number: ";
18      int x;
19      std::cin >> x;
20      if (doSomething(x) == ERROR_NEGATIVE_NUMBER)
21      {
22          std::cout << "You entered a negative number!\n";
23      }
24      else
25      {
26          std::cout << "It worked!\n";
27      }
28      return 0;
29  }
```

Switch statements

Switch statements are also no control statements that change the flow of control of the program. Switch statement uses the multi-way branch.

156

When compared to the 'if else if' statements, switch statements are superior because of the following reasons.

- Switch statements are easier to debug.
- These are easy to maintain
- Switch statements have a faster execution capacity
- There are easy to read
- The depth in case of the switch statement is fixed.
- Can be used for exception handling

The basic syntax of the switch statement is given below.

```
case constant1:
  code/s to be executed if n equals to
constant1;
  break;
case constant2:
  code/s to be executed if n equals to
constant2;
  break;
  .

  .
```

.

default:

code/s to be executed if n doesn't match to any cases;

The following program shows you why the switch case is easier to use when compared to the if-else statements.

Example:

```cpp
enum Colors
{
    COLOR_BLACK,
    COLOR_WHITE,
    COLOR_RED,
    COLOR_GREEN,
    COLOR_BLUE,
};
void PrintColor(Colors eColor)
{
    using namespace std;
    if (eColor == COLOR_BLACK)
        cout << "Black";
    else if (eColor == COLOR_WHITE)
        cout << "White";
    else if (eColor == COLOR_RED)
        cout << "Red";
    else if (eColor == COLOR_GREEN)
        cout << "Green";
    else if (eColor == COLOR_BLUE)
        cout << "Blue";
    else
        cout << "Unknown";
}
```

Now look at the same problem done using the switch statement.

```
1  ⊟void PrintColor(Colors eColor)
2  {
3      using namespace std;
4      switch (eColor)
5      {
6          case COLOR_BLACK:
7              cout << "Black";
8              break;
9          case COLOR_WHITE:
10             cout << "White";
11             break;
12         case COLOR_RED:
13             cout << "Red";
14             break;
15         case COLOR_GREEN:
16             cout << "Green";
17             break;
18         case COLOR_BLUE:
19             cout << "Blue";
20             break;
21         default:
22             cout << "Unknown";
23             break;
24     }
```

Break statement

We often use the break statement for terminating the case statement without the entire function been terminated. This will give an instruction to the compiler to abandon the current switch case and proceed with the execution of the next statement. So after a break statement the flow of control goes to the statement that is after the switch block. Here is an example showing the break statements attached after the case statements.

```
1  switch (2)
2  {
3      case 1: // Does not match -- skipped
4          cout << 1 << endl;
5          break;
6      case 2: // Match! Execution begins at the next statement
7          cout << 2 << endl; // Execution begins here
8          break; // Break terminates the switch statement
9      case 3:
10         cout << 3 << endl;
11         break;
12     case 4:
13         cout << 4 << endl;
14         break;
15     default:
16         cout << 5 << endl;
17         break;
18 }
```

Goto

For making the CPU to jump to a different spot in the code we make use of the flow control statement called the goto statement. For this we need to set a spot which we goto statement can identify it as a statement label. The following example if there is a negative number entered the goto statement will take the flow of control to the tryAgain label where they will have to choose nonnegative number.

Example 1:

```
1  #include <iostream>
2  #include <cmath>
3  int main()
4  {
5      using namespace std;
6  tryAgain: // this is a statement label
7      cout << "Enter a non-negative number";
8      double dX;
9      cin >> dX;
10     if (dX < 0.0)
11         goto tryAgain; // this is the goto statement
12     cout << "The sqrt of " << dX << " is " << sqrt(dX) << endl;
13 }
```

Example 2:

```
1  #include <iostream>
2  using namespace std;
3
4  int main ()
5  {
6      // Local variable declaration:
7      int a = 10;
8
9      // do loop execution
10 LOOP:do
11     {
12         if( a == 15)
13         {
14             // skip the iteration.
15             a = a + 1;
16             goto LOOP;
17         }
18         cout << "value of a: " << a << endl;
19         a = a + 1;
20     }while( a < 20 );
21
22     return 0;
23 }
```

While

Of all the three loops, while is the simplest of all. The while loop is very much similar to the 'if' statement. Here the condition will be given after the while statement. This will take the flow of control to the beginning of the program and will put it in a loop till the condition is satisfied.

Every time the loop goes back to the beginning after a successful execution of the code, it is said that and iteration is done.

Example:

```
1    // Loop through every number between 1 and 50
2    int iii = 1;
3    while (iii <= 50)
4    {
5        // print the number
6        cout << iii << " ";
7        // if the loop variable is divisible by 10, print a newline
8        if (iii % 10 == 0)
9            cout << endl;
10       // increment the loop counter
11       iii++;
12   }
```

The output will be:

```
1 2 3 4 5 6 7 8 9 10
11 12 13 14 15 16 17 18 19 20
21 22 23 24 25 26 27 28 29 30
31 32 33 34 35 36 37 38 39 40
41 42 43 44 45 46 47 48 49 50
```

Here is another simple example of a while loop.

```
1  #include <iostream>
2  using namespace std;
3
4  int main ()
5  {
6
7      int a = 10;
8
9      while( a < 20 )
10     {
11         cout << "value of a: " << a << endl;
12         a++;
13     }
14
15     return 0;
16  }
```

Output:

```
value of a: 10
value of a: 11
value of a: 12
value of a: 13
value of a: 14
value of a: 15
value of a: 16
value of a: 17
value of a: 18
value of a: 19
```

Like the 'if' condition, you can use a loop inside another loop. If you place a loop inside another loop it is called a nested loop.

Example of a nested loop:

```
1   // Loop between 1 and 5
2   int iii=1;
3   while (iii<=5)
4   {
5       // loop between 1 and iii
6       int jjj = 1;
7       while (jjj <= iii)
8           cout << jjj++;
9       // print a newline at the end of each row
10      cout << endl;
11      iii++;
12  }
```

The above program will display.

```
1
12
123
1234
12345
```

The do-while loop

The do-while loop is similar to the while loop except at one part. If the condition in the while loop is not satisfied, we know that it won't execute the loop. But if we want our code to run at least once even if the condition is not satisfied, we can make use of the do-while loop in C++. Using this loop will execute the code once even if the condition is not satisfied. Following example shows us the do-while loop.

```
1   #include <iostream>
2   int main()
3   {
4       using namespace std;
5       // nSelection must be declared outside do/while loop
6       int nSelection;
7       do
8       {
9           cout << "Please make a selection: " << endl;
10          cout << "1) Addition" << endl;
11          cout << "2) Subtraction" << endl;
12          cout << "3) Multiplication" << endl;
13          cout << "4) Division" << endl;
14          cin >> nSelection;
15      } while (nSelection != 1 && nSelection != 2 &&
16              nSelection != 3 && nSelection != 4);
17      // do something with nSelection here
18      // such as a switch statement
19      return 0;
20  }
```

For loop

The 'for' loop is the most widely used statement for looping in C++. This is a perfect option to use if you

163

know how many times to iterate. This is easy to use because it allows the user to change the variables after every iteration. This is really simple to use as you declare everything in a single go at the same place.

Here is a simple example for a 'for' loop.

Example 1:

```
1  #include<iostream>
2  #include<conio.h>
3
4  using namespace std;
5
6  int main()
7  {
8
9      // Variable Declaration
10     int a;
11
12     // Get Input Value
13     cout<<"Enter the Number :";
14     cin>>a;
15
16     //for Loop Block
17     for (int counter = 1; counter <= a; counter++)
18     {
19         cout<<"Execute "<<counter<<" time"<<endl;
20     }
21
22     getch();
23     return 0;
24 }
```

The output of the above code is:

```
Enter the Number :5
Execute 1 time
Execute 2 time
Execute 3 time
Execute 4 time
Execute 5 time
```

Example 2:

```
1  #include <iostream>
2  using namespace std;
3
4  int main()
5  {
6      int i, n, factorial = 1;
7      cout<<"Enter a positive integer: ";
8      cin>>n;
9      for (i = 1; i <= n; ++i) {
10         factorial *= i;    // factorial = factorial * i;
11     }
12     cout<< "Factorial of "<<n<<" = "<<factorial;
13     return 0;
14 }
```

Output:

Enter a positive integer: 4

Factorial of 4 is 24

Break and continue

We have already seen about the break statement in our previous examples. Here we will use break statement with the continue statement. We know that the break statement can be used to terminate this which statement and looping statements like while loop and do while loop. But when you use it with switch statement at the end of the function, it signifies that the case is completed or finished. Here is an example showing the combination of switch and a break.

Example:

```
1   switch (chChar)
2   {
3       case '+':
4           DoAddition(x, y);
5           break;
6       case '-':
7           DoSubtraction(x, y);
8           break;
9       case '*':
10          DoMultiplication(x, y);
11          break;
12      case '/':
13          DoDivision(x, y);
14          break;
15  }
```

When we use the break statement with a loop, we can terminate the loop early. The following example shows you how.

```
1   #include <cstdio> // for getchar()
2   #include <iostream>
3   using namespace std;
4   int main()
5   {
6       // count how many spaces the user has entered
7       int nSpaceCount = 0;
8       // loop 40 times
9       for (int nCount=0; nCount < 80; nCount++)
10      {
11          char chChar = getchar(); // read a char from user
12          // exit loop if user hits enter
13          if (chChar == '\n')
14              break;
15          // increment count if user entered a space
16          if (chChar == ' ')
17              nSpaceCount++;
18      }
19      cout << "You typed " << nSpaceCount << " spaces" << endl;
20      return 0;
21  }
```

In the above program, the user can type up to 40 characters. The loop can be terminated if the user presses the enter key. By pressing the enter key, the user can choose an early termination of the loop.

166

Continue statement

There will be situations where you will need to jump back to the beginning of the loop even earlier than the normal time. This can be useful for bypassing the rest of the loop for that iteration. The following example shows is the usage of the continue statement.

```
1   for (int iii=0; iii < 20; iii++)
2   {
3       // if the number is divisible by 4, skip this iteration
4       if ((iii % 4) == 0)
5           continue;
6       cout << iii << endl;
7   }
```

Here in the above program, we have used the continue statement with the for loop and it will print all the numbers between 0 and 19 that are not divisible by 4.

Using continue and break

Usually it is not advised to pair up continue with break. This is so because it will cause deviations in the flow of execution of the program code. But if used carefully, the continue and break combination can be proved efficient. Here is a small example showing it.

```
1   int nPrinted = 0;
2   for (int iii=0; iii < 100; iii++)
3   {
4       // if the number is divisible by 3 or 4, skip this iteration
5       if ((iii % 3)==0 || (iii % 4)==0)
6           continue;
7       cout << iii << endl;
8       nPrinted++;
9   }
10  cout << nPrinted << " numbers were found" << endl;
```

Random number generation

Some programs will need to generate random numbers. A computer cannot generate a random number on its own unless you give it a certain code to execute. These random numbers are particularly used in programs related to statistics and games. Games like online poker or dice rolling games use a random number generation algorithm for generating random numbers.

What fun would it be if a game keeps on generating the same numbers for every player? And for machines like computers which know only values that are either true or false, cannot generate these random numbers on their own. For such cases, we use the pseudo random number generator algorithms. Here, the computer will take a random number which is actually a non-random number called the seed, and performs mathematical operations to transform the given seed into a different number which seems to be random.

Efficient random number generators will continue to execute the process over and over and will generate a number that is completely unrelated to the seed. These random numbers are also used in ATM machines for security purposes.

Generating a pseudo random number is not that hard. Here you'll understand it with the following example. This program generates 100 pseudo random numbers.

```cpp
#include <stdafx.h>
#include <iostream>
using namespace std;
unsigned int PRNG()
{
    // our initial starting seed is 5323
    static unsigned int nSeed = 5323;
    // Take the current seed and generate a new value from it
    // Due to our use of large constants and overflow, it would be
    // very hard for someone to predict what the next number is
    // going to be from the previous one.
    nSeed = (8253729 * nSeed + 2396403);
    // Take the seed and return a value between 0 and 32767
    return nSeed % 32767;
}
int main()
{
    // Print 100 random numbers
    for (int nCount=0; nCount < 100; ++nCount)
    {
        cout << PRNG() << "\t";
        // If we've printed 5 numbers, start a new column
        if ((nCount+1) % 5 == 0)
            cout << endl;
    }
}
```

Output

```
6474  76890 753   0973  4582  3451  4597  5489  3407  866
6547  85421 87    7430  478   3457  496   148   04432 6432
9350  6512  8744  987   3432  0923  6570  34109 56    34998
6430  77665 09332 76233 06077 6755  6     67733 8766  0981
398   4576  0278  4650  8746  3508  7586  4756  927   356
359   2354  9125  39    715   2397  12    978   612   645
361   87236 417   8236  4781  6239  478   3416  44395 7164
9571  69    4561  947   5619  4563  348   09997 67443 09453
6354  8615  2348  1523  8451  26753 547   67596 7863  6558
651   9645  1963  549   1549  1235  3487  89543 9966  080
```

You can see that from the above output, all the numbers are random and there is no relation between them. If there was any, that would be random too.

You can actually generate random numbers in C++ by using the built in pseudo a random number generator. Here, you will make use of two functions. They are srand() and rand().

srand() will set the initial value or in other words, the seed value. While the rand() takes the srand() value and will start generating random numbers basing on the srand() value. You can understand it better with the following example.

```cpp
#include <stdafx.h>
#include <iostream>
#include <cstdlib> // for rand() and srand()
using namespace std;
int main()
{
    srand(53); // set initial seed value to 53
    // Print 100 random numbers
    for (int nCount=0; nCount < 100; ++nCount)
    {
        cout << rand() << "\t";
        // If we've printed 5 numbers, start a new column
        if ((nCount+1) % 5 == 0)
            cout << endl;
    }
}
```

This will generate 100 random numbers

```
746    5107  3640  5716  3405  610   3475  6017  4650  1873
46530  8173  465   9871  34560 14765 01746 50187 4650  8174
6508   1746  5846  5198  3476  891   4376  139   84758 3947
6591   287   364   2019  54865 58465 8686  544   99876 445
4555   6654  0987  3432  67778 984   65465 786   3540  8777
4591   5941  5294  651   4194  581   26354 912   6359  421
653    4961  25394 7167  459   1539  1365  6512  9364  5197
2359   1625  3958  7142  6051  8645  0871  3469  6123  5978
61304  9861  8855  4455  9865  0553  6678  65432 9554  4522
3442   436   6534  3653  653   6536  56476 576   5533  6522
```

Hear from the about generated random numbers, you can see that no number is less than the srand() value given. That is because that value is taken as the base and the other numbers are generated from it.

Chapter 12: Programming Languages and Creating a Program

This chapter will be about the actual task of creating your own program. The information contained within this chapter won't end up being a series of step-by-step directions on what exactly you need to do at every turn, as these steps will be different and will vary depending on the kind of programming language that you are using and the kind of program that you want to create. However, it will be going over all of the things that you should consider and all of the information that you will need to know when you are approaching the idea of creating a program of your own. As with all of the topics that have been and will be discussed in this book, it is strongly encouraged that you do some additional research of your own beyond what you read here in order to gain a more complete understanding of the concepts and ideas that will be gone over here.

The first step to creating your own program, of course, is to learn a programming language. Anyone who wants to be able to develop their own software, whether that software will take the form of a game, program, or even another type of service, has to be able to express the commands and instructions in a way that will be "understood" by the computers that will end up receiving them in order to carry out those commands and instructions. This means that you should be familiar with the language that you will be using when creating your program. There are a very large number of different programming languages that are all good for different things, so it is, again, very strongly advised that you do your own research on these languages in order to choose which one you think will be able to provide the most utility to you. It is important to take into account the kinds of programs that you wish to create or work on, as well, and which features that you would like to include within them as well. This is not exactly a comprehensive list, but some helpful examples of a few programming languages and their specific advantages are:

- C++, which is typically used in game development and graphics compilers
- C#, which is most commonly used for the development of web apps and Enterprise Cross-Applications Development
- Java, which is commonly used in the development of web applications and Android applications, as well as desktop applications and games

- Python, which is used for a number of purposes, such as Desktop GUIs, Scientific and numeric applications, and web applications, but most commonly for the development of Artificial Intelligence and Machine Learning.
- R, which can be useful for statistical computing and data projects, as well as for machine learning
- *Swift is a programming language that was developed by Apple, Inc., for the development of Apple's Cocoa and Cocoa Touch frameworks to create iOS apps.*

The programming language that you will use will need to be heavily dependent on the specific kind of program that you intend to create. Because of this, you should try to have a good idea of the kind of program that you want to create beforehand. This can be a very important thing for you to consider. Do you want to create games, mobile applications, or do you exclusively want to work with Apple devices? These kinds of questions can be very important to answer very early on. In order to do this, you should try to gain a good understanding of your goals.

Once you understand the general goals that you have, you might be struggling to find a more specific target. Maybe you know you want to create something that will be useful and that will be easy for users to understand. Maybe you've had it with that outdated social media platform that everyone seems to deal with out of lack of an alternative. Or maybe you have no idea where to start. Either way, you might want to try to brainstorm to come up with good ideas. You might want to take a look at the software that is currently available to you, that you think could be better or that doesn't do its job very well. How would you make that task go a little bit more smoothly, or how would you handle it differently? Another way to accomplish this is to take a look at the things that you use your computer to do on a daily basis. Is there an issue somewhere? Something that you wish would be a little bit easier or that you could automate, either in part or as a whole? You should be making a point to write all of these ideas down and taking note of them as much as you can. It can also be important, however, to start simple. You might want to start off with smaller projects and grow and develop your skills over time. You will be able to learn and grow much more efficiently if you are able to set clear, tangible goals for yourself that you can see yourself being able to reach, and starting off with a very large long-term goal can be intimidating especially for a beginner.

Once you have finished with this step, you should move on to making a decision on an editor. An editor is any type of program that can allow you to write and store computer code. These programs can take the form of a number of different kinds of things, like a simple text editor or notepad application, to more complex and advances programs, such as Microsoft Visual Studio, Adobe Dreamweaver, or JDeveloper. Technically, you can write any kind of program in a simple text editor such as your computer's "notepad" application, which means that it is absolutely possible to get started with computer programming for free, with no extra work spent on the resources and tools that you might need in order to start working on your projects. However, it is highly recommended that you use a more advanced editor to learn on, and especially to develop your own projects with, especially as you become a little bit more comfortable with your chosen programming language. A good editor can serve to make the process of writing code and being able to test that code much easier and much more efficient, which will, in turn, help you to get more coding done more quickly! A few good examples of editors that you might want to use are Notepad ++ if you are on a windows computer. Notepad ++ is completely free and additionally, it has the capability for "syntax highlighting", as well. For Mac users, the free editor called "TextEdit" is recommended, for similar reasons. Additionally, it can be useful to note that certain visual programming languages, such as visual basic, don't require any additional tools, as they include their editor and compiler in one package due to the nature of the languages that they deal with.

The next thing that you will want to consider is the compiler that you use. Most commonly used computer programming languages are considered to be "high level" programming languages. This means that the language will be very easy for you, the user, to understand, but will also be difficult or impossible for your computer to understand. In order for the computer to be able to understand the instructions that are being given to it through that language, your program will need to be "compiled", or interpreted. Of course, not all languages require a compiler in order for your computer to be able to understand them, so usually, the programming language that you choose to use will decide whether or not you need a compiler to "translate" or interpret your code in the language that it has been written in. For example, Java needs to be translated by a compiler into a format that your computer is able to understand, while other languages like "Perl" are already interpreted, which means that your computer is already able to understand it and code written in the "Perl" language does not need to be compiled. Instead, languages like this one simply need to be installed on the computer or the server that is running the script.

Once you have made a decision on the specific programming language that you will use, you simply need to learn that language. The easiest and simplest place for most people to start is the classic "Hello, World!" program. This is a simple program that is usually taught to beginners, which prints the phrase "Hello, World!" onto the screen. Once you are able to produce this simple code, the next step is to learn the ins and outs of the syntax of your chosen language. In order to do this, there are a few concepts and ideas that can be helpful to learn.

The first of these very important skills is to learn how to "declare variables". The declaration of a variable, in computer programming, is the simple act of assigning, or "declaring", a particular variable for future use. You will need to provide a type of data and a name for the variable when it is being declared. You can also request that a specific value is placed within the variable, as well. In a language like Java, which is a high-level language, the programmer can simply declare the variable and move onward. The computer's hardware will simply provide the information that has been requested when it becomes relevant, and the details and specifics will be up to the compiler that you are using. When the program starts, the variable will have the value that has been requested stored in it already. It is also important to note that it is not possible for a variable to be used within a specific program unless it has already been declared, as well.

Another useful thing to understand will be the "if/else" statement. This can be a very easy concept to understand, as it is simply a way to make a decision based on different inputs. You might have to make a decision between two options, such as "should I turn left or right?" or "should I eat one cookie or two?" The ways that you make decisions about these kinds of questions are very similar to the ways that computers make these kinds of decisions, as well. You might say "Well, I'll ask my friend. If they want to meet up, I'll go left to meet with them. If not, then I'll just turn right to go home." or "If there are more than 10 cookies left, then I'll have two. Otherwise, I'll just have one". These are both excellent examples of if/else statements. The basic idea behind the if/else statement is that they are presented as ways of making "decisions" about a particular thing based on various external factors or inputs. These statements can be expressed in the code as something similar to this line of "pseudocode":

```
If (more than 10 cookies) {

Take two

} else {

Take one

}
```

In this simple line of fake code, the example of the cookies is used to express how an if/else statement works. The decision that is made is based on a "test" of the number of cookies that are in the cookie jar. Usually, these statements will be testing whether one value is larger or smaller than another value or whether the value exists at all. These factors will then be used to influence the "decision" that is made. If the test fails, then the alternative option will be carried out. In this case, you will get one cookie instead of two, due to the limited availability of the cookies. These functions can also be expressed as flowcharts and can be stacked within and on top of other conditional statements for more complex decisions. The conditional, "if/else" statement is one of the most useful aspects of computer programming.

Another type of function that can be helpful to learn is the "for" loop. The "for" loop goes through a list and processes each item in that list, applying them to a "loop" in sequence. Each item in the list is reassigned to the loop variable, and the loop is then executed. The typical form that a loop variable will take is:

"For "loop variable" in "sequence":

Statements

The loop variable is only created whenever the "for" statement is run, so there is no need for you to create the variable before that point. Each item in the sequence is assigned to the loop variable in each iteration of the loop and is executed when they have been completed. This statement is finished as soon as the final item in the sequence has been reached. This might look something like:

```
for reader in ['reader 1', 'reader 2', 'reader 3']:

    book = "Hello " + reader + ". Please read my book."

    print(book)
```

Another very simple tool that you can use is the comment. A comment can be described as a simple annotation or "comment" that a programmer can place into the source code of a program as a short note to themselves or anyone else who might be viewing the comment. These can make code much easier for you to understand and read quickly, by leaving comments telling yourself or any other reader what a specific line of code is meant to do. These comments will be visible to you as the reader, but will usually be ignored or "invisible" to a compiler or interpreter. In JavaScript, this will be "//", however, the form that it takes will differ between different programming languages. You should find out what the trigger is for the language that you are using. The comment can be a very useful tool for organization and generally understanding the programs that you write and should be implemented into your code as often as you can remember to do so.

Chapter 13: Common Programming Challenges

The excitement about programming can fizzle out fast and turn into a nightmare. There are unexpected challenges that might make life difficult for you, especially as a beginner programmer. However, these challenges should not set you back or kill your resolve. They are common challenges that a lot of people have experienced before, and they overcame them, as you will too.

If you want to succeed in programming, you should be aware of the fact that mistakes do happen, and you will probably make many of them. The downside of mistakes is that you can feel you are not good enough. Everyone else seems to be doing fine, but not you. On the flip side, mistakes are an opportunity for you to learn and advance.

No one was born as good as they are today. What we are is the sum of mistakes and learning from those mistakes and experience. Feel free to reach out to mentors whenever you feel stuck. Deadlines and bug reports might overwhelm you, but once you get the hang of it, you will do great.

The following are some common challenges that you might experience as a beginner programmer.

Debugging

You feel content with a project, satisfied that it will run without a hitch and perform the desired duties. However, when you arrive at your desk in the morning, your quality assurance team has other ideas. They point out what seem like endless issues with the project. Perhaps the *OK* button is not responsive, the error messages are not displaying correctly and so forth.

All these are issues that eventually leave a negative impact on the user experience. You must get back to the drawing board and figure out where the problem lies. Debugging will be part of your life as a programmer. It is not enjoyable, but it is the reality.

Debugging is one of the most exhausting things you have to do. If you are lucky, you will encounter bugs that can be fixed easily. Most of the time, debugging costs you hours, and lots of coffee. However, do not feel downtrodden yet. Bugs are all over the place in programming. Even the best code you will ever come across needs debugging at some point.

Solution

How do you handle the debugging process and make your life easier? The first step is to document your work. Documentation might seem like a lot of work for you, but it helps you trace your steps in the event of an error. That way, you can easily trace the source and fix it, saving you from inspecting hundreds or thousands of code.

Another way of making light work of debugging is to recreate the problem. You must understand what the problem is before you try to solve it. If you recreate the problem, you isolate it from the rest of the code and get a better perspective of it.

Talk to someone. You might not always have all the answers. Do not fear anyone, especially if you work in a team. Beginner programmers often feel some people are out of reach, perhaps because of the positions they hold. However, if you do not ask for help, you will never really know whether the person will be helpful or not. The best person to ask for help, for example, is the quality tester who identified the problem, especially if you are unable to recreate the problem.

Working smart

As a programmer, one thing you must be aware of is that you will be sitting down for hours on end working on some code. This becomes your normal routine. You, however, are aware of the risks this poses to your health. Neck sprains, numb legs, back pain, pain in your palms and fingers from typing away all day. For a beginner, you might not be ready for the challenge yet. However, you must still dig in daily to meet your deliverables.

Solution

The first thing you must consider is regular exercise. If you work a desk job, it is possible to lose motivation and feel exhausted even before your workday is over. You can tackle this by keeping a workout routine. Jog before you go to work every morning, take a brisk half-hour walk and so forth. There are many simple routines that you can initiate which will help you handle the situation better.

While at work, take some time off and walk around— without looking like you are wasting time. This helps to relieve your body of the pain and pressure, and more importantly, allows for proper blood circulation. Other than that, you do not have to keep typing while seated.

Stand up from time to time. Some companies have invested in height-adjustable desks, which help with this.

User experience

One of the most common challenges you will experience as a programmer is managing user experiences. You will come across a lot of clients in the course of your programming career. However, not all clients know how to communicate their needs. As a result, you will be involved in a lot of back and forth on project details and deliverables.

Most users have a good idea of what they need the project you are developing to do. However, this is not always the same as what your development team believes. Given that most beginner programmers never interact directly with the clients, especially in a team project, it might be difficult for you to understand them.

Solution

The best way around this is to figure out the best features of the project. Your client already knows what they want the project to do. Ask the right questions, especially to members of your team who are in direct contact with the client or the end user. The best responses will often come from designers and user experience experts. Their insight comes from interacting with users most of the time.

Another option is to test the product you are designing. You have probably used test versions of some products in the past. Most major players in the tech industry release beta versions of their products before the final. This way, users try it out, share their views, ideas and challenges they encounter. This information is collected and used to refine the beta product before the final one is released.

Testing your product allows you to identify and fix bugs before you release the product to the end user. It also allows you to interact with the user and gauge the level of acceptance for your project.

Estimates

A lot of beginner programmers struggle with scheduling. Perhaps you gave an estimate for a task and are unable to meet it. You are now a professional. Never delude yourself that you are not, perhaps because you are a beginner. This industry focuses on deadlines a lot. In software development, estimates are crucial. They are often used to plan bigger schedules for projects, and in some cases agree on the project quotes. Delays end up in problems that might in the long run affect trust between the parties involved.

Solution

The first step towards getting your estimates right is to apportion time properly. Time management is key. Set out a schedule within which you can complete a given task. Within that schedule, allow yourself ample buffer time for any inconvenience, but not too much time. For example, allow yourself 30-40 minutes for an assignment that should take 20 minutes.

Another way of improving your scheduling challenges is to break down assignments into micro milestones. A series of small tasks is easier to manage. Besides, when you complete these micro assignments, you are more psyched about getting onto the next one, and so on. You end up with a lighter workload which is also a good way to prevent burnout.

Constant updates

The tech industry keeps expanding in leaps and bounds. You can barely go a month before you learn about some groundbreaking work. Everything keeps upgrading or updating to better, more efficient versions. Libraries, tools and frameworks are not left behind either. Updates are awesome. Most updates improve user experiences, and bolster the platform security. However, updates come with undue pressure, even for the most experienced programmers out there.

Solution

Stay abreast with the latest developments in your field of expertise. You cannot know everything, but catching up on trends from time to time will help you learn some new tools and tips available, which can also help you improve on your skills and develop cutting edge products.

Another option is to learn. The beauty of the world of IT is that things are always changing. It is one of the most dynamic industries today. Carve out half an hour daily to learn something new. You will be intrigued by how much you will have mastered after a few weeks. In your spare time, challenge yourself to build something simple, solve a problem and so forth. There are lots of challenge websites available today where you can have a go at real-world problems.

Problems communicating

Beginner programmers face the communication challenge all the time. You are new to the workplace, so you do not really know anyone. Most of the team members and managers are alien to you, and as a result you often feel out of place. At some point in time every programmer goes through this. You feel like a baby among giants. Eventually, the pressure gets to you and you make a grave mistake, which could have been avoided if you reached out to someone to assist.

Solution

Dealing with communication problems is more than just a social interaction concern. First, you must learn to be proactive. If something bugs you, ask for help. The worst that can happen is people might laugh, especially if it is a rookie question, but someone will go out of their way and help you. If they don't and something goes awry, the department shoulders the blame for their ignorance. Before you know it, people will keep checking in on you to make sure you are getting it right, and you might also make some good friends in the process.

Consistency is another way to handle the communication challenge. For a beginner, you might not always get everything right. These are moments you can learn from. With practice, you grow bolder and learn to express yourself better over time.

Security concerns

Data is the new gold. This is the reality of the world right now. Data is precious, and is one of the reasons why tech giants are facing lawsuits all over the place. Huawei recently found themselves in a spat with the US government that ended up in a host of severed ties. There are so many reasons behind the hard stance that the US government took against Huawei, and most of them circle back to data.

People are willing to pay a great deal of money to access specific data that can benefit them in one way or the other. Some companies play the short-term game, others are in it for the long-term. Competitors also use nefarious ways to gain access to their competitors' databases and see what they are working on, and how they do it.

As a programmer, one thing your clients expect from you is that their data is safe, and the data their clients share with them through your project. Beginner programmers are fairly aware of all the security risks involved. This should not worry you so much, especially if you are part of a team of able developers. They will always have contingency measures in place. However, you must not be ignorant of security loopholes, especially in your code.

Solution

Hackers are always trying to gain access to some code. You cannot stop them from trying. You can, however, make it difficult for them to penetrate your code. Give them a challenge. The single biggest threat to any secure platform is human interaction. At times your code will not be compromised by someone from outside, but someone you know. In most cases, they compromise your code without knowing they do—unless they did it intentionally.

Make sure your workstation is safe. Every time you step away from your workstation, ensure your screen is locked, and if you are going away for a long time, shut down your devices.

In your programming language, it is also advisable that you use parameterized queries especially for SQL injections. This is important because most hackers use SQL injections to gain access and steal information.

Relying on foreign code

You have written some code for a few years and believe in your ability. You are confident you are good enough, hence being hired by the company. However, make peace with the fact that you will have to work on projects that were written by someone else. Working with another person's code is not always an easy thing, especially if their code seems outdated. There is a reason why the company insists on using that particular code.

The worst possible situation would be company politics–they occur everywhere. Someone wrote some code which the entire company relies on, but you cannot change or question it because the original coder has some connection with the company hierarchy. Often this raises a problem where you are unable to figure out the code.

Solution

Since there is not much you can do about the code, why not try to learn it? If you can, talk to the developer who wrote it and understand their reasoning behind it. This way, it is easier for you to embrace their style, and you will also have a smooth time handling your projects. You never know, you might just show them something new and help them rethink their code.

Another option is to embrace this code. It is not yours, but it is what you have and will be using for a very long time. Change your attitude about that code. Take responsibility for the code and work with it. This way, your hesitation will slowly fade away.

Lack of planning

While you have a burning desire to impress in your new place of work, you must have a plan. Many beginner programmers do not. Many programmers jump into writing code before stopping in their tracks to determine the direction they want to steer the code. The problem with this approach is that you will fail to make sense. The code might sound right in your head, but on paper nothing works.

Solution

Conceptualize an idea. Everything starts with an idea. Say you want to write a program that allows users to share important calendar dates and milestones with their loved ones. Focusing on this idea helps you remember why you are writing that code.

Once you have an idea, how do you connect it with real problems? What are the problems you are trying to solve? How are they connected to your idea? This also begs the question—why do people need your program?

Planning will help you save time when writing a program, and at the same time, help you stay on track.

Finally

In programming, everyone starts somewhere. Being the new person in the company should not scare you. Communicate with your peers and seniors, be willing to learn from them, and all the things that might seem overwhelming will somehow become easier as time goes by.

Conclusion

Thank you again for purchasing this book! I hope you enjoyed reading it as much as I enjoyed writing it for you!

Keep in mind that, if you have any questions that may not have been answered in this book, you can always visit the Python website! The Python website contains a lot of material that will help you work with Python and ensure that you are entering your code properly. You can also find any updates that you may need for your Python program in the event that your program is not updating properly or you need another version of it.

Python works with Machine Learning, as you have discovered, because you are teaching the Python program to execute the code that you want to be executed. Most likely, you won't work with unsupervised learning with Python unless you are working with infinite loops. Remember, however, that you should use infinite loops sparingly!

You can work with the program and teach it what you want it to do, and you may even be able to help someone else out if they are not able to get the program to do what they want it to do!

Just remember that you do not need to worry if your Python code doesn't work the first time because using Python takes a lot of practice. The more you practice, the better your code will look, and the better it will be executed. Not only that, but you will get to see Machine Learning in action each time you enter your code!

www.ingramcontent.com/pod-product-compliance
Lightning Source LLC
Chambersburg PA
CBHW071119050326
40690CB00008B/1272